# GHOST INVESTIGATOR

## Volume 7
## Psychic Impressions

### Written by
# Linda Zimmermann

A
Spirited
Books
Publication

Also by Linda Zimmermann

Bad Astronomy
Forging a Nation
Civil War Memories
Ghosts of Rockland County
Haunted Hudson Valley
More Haunted Hudson Valley
Haunted Hudson Valley III
A Funny Thing Happened on the Way to Gettysburg
Rockland County: Century of History
Mind Over Matter
Home Run
Ghost Investigator, Volume 1: Hauntings of the Hudson Valley
Ghost Investigator, Volume 2: From Gettysburg, PA to Lizzie Borden, AX
Ghost Investigator, Volume 3
Dead Center
Rockland County Scrapbook
Ghost Investigator, Volume 4: Ghosts of New York and New Jersey
Ghost Investigator, Volume 5: From Beyond the Grave
Ghost Investigator, Volume 6: Dark Shadows

The author is always looking for new ghost stories. If you would like to share a haunting experience go to:

www.ghostinvestigator.com

Or write to:

Linda Zimmermann
P.O. Box 192
Blooming Grove, NY 10914

Or send email to:
linda@gotozim.com

Ghost Investigator: Volume 7
Copyright © 2007 Linda Zimmermann

ISBN: 978-0-9799002-0-4

# CONTENTS

# Introduction

2007 has just been a completely awful year. Both of my beloved dogs, Dini and Shadow, succumbed to cancer, followed by my father-in-law, and I continue to feel their loss every hour of the day. I am simply not the same person anymore without them, and I doubt I ever will be. Many other terrible things have also occurred, to the point where it has been difficult to find relief from the tragedies I deal with in ghost investigations. Both the living and the dead are unhappy these days.

They say that whatever doesn't kill you makes you stronger, but I have a few choice words about that ridiculous idea. As the cases in this book illustrate, whatever doesn't kill you can make your life miserable, and that misery can drift over into death. Suicides, murders, physical and mental illnesses are the recipes for a haunting, and regret, remorse, and suffering are the ingredients.

It is not by coincidence that three of the stories involve suicides (and two on the same street!); one is about an old hotel where death came in many tragic forms, while another deals with a restaurant where jealousy may have led to murder. In addition, almost all of them involve terrible diseases, both physical and mental, that brought great suffering to the victims and their families.

What lesson can be learned from all this? There is really no good way to die, but there are good ways to live. As you read these stories in the seventh volume of the *Ghost Investigator* series, realize that every decision you make is important and can have long lasting repercussions. I've said this many times, but it's worth repeating— don't live a life of regret; find the courage to make the changes that will make your life happier. If you do, you will probably give future ghost hunters one less case to investigate.

All of this gloom and misery aside, I have chosen to name this book *Psychic Impressions,* as the sixth sense aspect continues to play an ever important role in my work. Starting with psychic Cyra Green's remarkable results in two previous cases, to the amazing work of Lisa Ann (www.spiritquesthealingcenter.com) in several of this year's investigations, to the ongoing and deepening impressions that fellow ghost hunter Mike Worden and myself experience, the intuitive senses continue to prove to be a valuable tool.

I still strive to obtain documented scientific and historical evidence, but I cannot deny that there is valuable information that can be obtained through psychic impressions—information that often couldn't be found with any traditional methods. Like everything else, however, it is a tool that must be used properly, and with frequent reality checks. The imagination can play tricks, especially in dark, creepy places, so just be on guard and try to verify everything, if possible.

That being said, I think you will see that in these stories, mere imagination can't account for what was found and verified. As always, I leave it up to you to decide whether or not you believe, but please keep an open mind, and remember that I painstakingly try to relate everything exactly as it happened.

With that, there are some people to thank.

My husband, Bob Strong, continues to give his support to all of my crazy endeavors, both personal and work related. Police Detective Michael Worden is always willing and able to help in investigations—even if they require long road trips with lots of brownies. He has started his own website, so please drop him a line to encourage him to finish his first book (www.paranormalpolice.com).

Many thanks to psychic Lisa Ann, who has been "dead on" with her abilities at several haunted locations, providing vital information. Thanks and hugs also to Barbara Bleitzhofer for both her psychic abilities and organizational skills. And as always, my gratitude to all the people in this book, both named and anonymous, who have let me into their homes and businesses to explore the paranormal realm firsthand.

I hope you all enjoy these stories, but before you continue, I have one favor to ask. Say a little prayer for Dini and Shadow, and any pets or people you may have lost this past year. The mind has amazing powers to influence this world and the next, as you will understand when you experience your own psychic impressions…

Linda Zimmermann
August 2007

**Special thanks** to Cindy and Sal Nicosia, and
Barbara Bleitzhofer, pictured inside the
beautifully restored Shanley Hotel.
See story, page 30.

# A Life of Regret
## Liberty, NY

In 2004, I investigated a house built in 1885 in Liberty, NY, and the fascinating story of its haunted activity appeared in *Ghost Investigator, Volume 4*. To summarize, with excerpts from that story:

In October of 1998, Cheryl's sister bought a large Victorian home in Liberty, New York. Cheryl, her husband, Dan, and their four-year-old daughter, Aarron, moved into the second story of the house. The winter passed quietly, with no sign that there was anything out of the ordinary. Then in the spring of 1999, Aarron came running out of the playroom, yelling that there was a woman in the closet. Cheryl rushed into the room, but found no one. She repeatedly assured Aarron that there wasn't anyone in the playroom, but the girl refused to go back in the room for the rest of the day. The young girl also began complaining about "lights" in her room at night that would keep her awake.

Bizarre occurrences were not limited to the upstairs portion of this house. Strange things also happened to Cheryl's sister on the first floor. On several occasions while taking a shower, she has heard children laughing and running up and down the stairs. At first, she assumed it was Cheryl's kids (they had added a son, named Justin), but each time she discovered that no one else was at home.

One afternoon she called Cheryl and was somewhat annoyed, wanting to know what had been going on upstairs all day, as for hours it sounded like the kids had been jumping up and down making a tremendous racket. Cheryl calmly replied that they had just gotten home, and the upstairs had been empty all day. It appears that if a woman's spirit does haunt the house, she has a few boisterous children to keep her company.

As disconcerting as it must be to hear phantom children, imagine what it must be like to actually *see* one—or worse yet, to be *touched* by a tiny hand reaching across the void between life and death. Unfortunately for Cheryl, the unthinkable happened to her one day when she least expected it. She had just come home after dropping off her daughter and nieces at Girl Scouts. She carried Justin to the second floor, put him down on the couch in the living room, and turned to close the childproof gate at the top of the stairs.

Apparently, another spiritual gateway was open at the time, and at least one child had already slipped through, because there beside her was standing a blond little boy. He reached out his hand and quickly tapped her back as if playing a game of tag.

An icy jolt raced up Cheryl's back, and her hair literally stood on end. She could hardly believe her eyes, but there was a boy, as real and solid as a living child. And that touch of his hand—a solid touch, but not like anything from the world of the living. This contact with the dead had a stunning effect. Cheryl admits that she "freaked" and ran down the hall. She immediately called her father, and for half an hour he gently urged her to take deep breaths and try to calm down.

When Dan came home, Cheryl told him all about her unearthly encounter, and how the chill in her spine from the little boy's touch was still with her. Despite all that had already occurred in the house, Dan kind of shrugged off the encounter, understandably finding it hard to believe that a dead child had materialized in his home, played tag with his wife and then vanished. However, he would undergo a very rapid change in attitude about one week later.

He and Cheryl were sitting in the kitchen, and he had a clear view of the hallway. As they spoke, he saw something move out of the corner of his eye, and turned to see a little boy run down the hall and turn into Justin's room. Dan told his wife what he just saw, and she said it couldn't have been Justin, as he was in the living room watching television. Determined to prove his wife wrong, Dan went into his son's room, but found it empty. He then went into the living room and found Justin watching television, as he had been during the time some other little boy was running down the hall.

Another unusual manifestation occurred late one night in the living room (which always feels cold, even during the summer). Cheryl had fallen asleep on the couch, but was awakened by something about 2am. There in the corner of the room was a wedding dress, floating in mid-air. Several times she closed her eyes and rubbed them, but each time when she opened them, the wedding dress was still there. She described the dress as a turn-of-century style with "poofy" sleeves, perhaps from the era when the house was first built. As she stared at the dress, wondering what else might appear or happen, it simply faded from sight.

2

As if all this wasn't enough to live with, there is also a temporary grave marker in the basement. It was for a woman named Mary, and for some reason activity in the house always greatly increased whenever that marker is moved.

Over the past few years, I would occasionally hear from Cheryl and was pleased to learn that things were relatively quiet. That all changed in September, 2006.

Justin was now 6 years-old, and by all accounts he was a normal, well-adjusted boy. Then one night he left his bedroom and went into the living room to sleep. The next night he got up and again went to the couch. The following night he began to get very agitated at bedtime, not wanting to even go into his bedroom. When this behavior continued, Cheryl asked what on earth was wrong. Justin's answer was startling.

He explained that two children came into his room every night and they would wake him up because they wanted to play. There was a little boy who was very energetic, and a younger girl who was more shy and quiet. The boy would jump on the bed, poke him, and do whatever he could to get Justin to play.

He further explained that the little boy often played too rough, frightening the girl, who would flee to the living room. Justin repeatedly asked the boy to leave him alone so he could sleep, but the boy wouldn't stop, forcing him to also go into the living room to get some peace and quiet.

It was an interesting story, but one that was well within the realm of the imagination of a six-year-old boy. Of course, as the spirits of children were known to haunt this house, Cheryl and Dan had to consider that this might be more than just a case of imaginary friends. Weeks passed, and Justin became even more reluctant to enter his room at night, and his description of the rambunctious boy and shy girl remained consistent. Then one night at bedtime he burst into tears and pleaded with Cheryl not to make him sleep in his room. Only after agreeing to let him keep his TV and light on, did he relent and go to bed.

When Cheryl sent me the first email about her son waking up in the middle of the night, I had to make sure there weren't other factors involved. Had he ever had problems before? Did he drink soda containing caffeine at night? Could there be any other health or nutritional explanations? It's always important to rule out any natural causes before considering the paranormal, and when this didn't seem to be a case of a natural sleep disorder, it appeared as though another investigation would be warranted.

At the time, I was in the midst of my busy lecture season and was hoping that things would remain stable at the house long enough to get past it, but then I received another email from Cheryl that contained the following:

"Well, we have gone from Justin not sleeping at night to not going to bed unless we promise to keep his DVD/TV on all night. He cries if I tell him that I plan on shutting it off during the night because he doesn't want Jack to come in his room anymore. I've never had a bad experience in this house and I don't know why my son is so afraid. He tells me that all Jack and Jill want to do is play, but I've never seen him so frightened to go to bed. He doesn't even go in there to play! We have got to do something. I need to know who these kids are and why they are attached to my son and yet leave my daughter alone. Justin should feel happy in his own home, not nervous and upset! HELP!"

Apparently the spirits were very restless and were not about to wait.

I contacted Mike and psychic Lisa Ann, and we arranged to visit the Liberty house ASAP. It was a cold Friday morning when we arrived at the large Victorian home. I had instructed Cheryl and Dan not to reveal anything to Lisa Ann about what was going on, and I hadn't told her anything, either, other than this promised to be an interesting case.

She later told me that she did have some concern that I was bringing her to another oppressively negative haunting like the one in Pomona, NY (with the dark figure, see *GI V6*), so when we pulled into the driveway she was pleasantly surprised that she wasn't met by a wave of evil.

However, she was met by something equally bizarre, albeit benign. As we got out of the car, Lisa Ann looked up at the house and saw an old woman looking out at her from the attic window. Of course, there weren't any old women in the house, at least not of the living variety, and Dan explained that it isn't even possible to stand up in front of that window due to the low rafters.

Before exploring the inside of the house, Lisa Ann was drawn to the backyard where she sensed flowing water and someone being pushed. There is indeed a stream behind the house, with a steep and dangerous embankment. Whoever had been pushed had been seriously

4

injured, but she did not feel that the victim was connected with the house, or that any ghosts were involved. Instead, it was the residue of the fear of falling that still hung in the air after many years. That residual fear may actually seep into the house, as Cheryl had previously reported that she frequently felt afraid of falling down the main staircase!

The attic window where Lisa Ann saw an old woman standing.

As we entered the top level of the two-family house, Lisa Ann confirmed the presence of an old woman, a very sad old woman. A few moments later, she added that she heard the "pitter-patter" of feet—the little feet of children running up and down the hallways. They were not negative entities, just very energetic and they loved to play.

Talk about batting a thousand! While I was tempted to shout, "That's it!" and give her a high five, I played it cool and didn't say she was wrong or right. We had only been in the house a few minutes, and I didn't want to influence the remainder of the investigation.

We moved from room to room, and when we went into Justin's bedroom Lisa Ann immediately said that this was where the children were most active. She went on to say that there were two children, close in age. I asked if they were male or female, and she said there is a boy and a girl.

Right again!

"Okay," I said plainly, still not letting on that she was reading the activity in the house like an open book.

Justin's bed, where the spirit of a little boy liked to play.

On the first floor of the house, the presence of the children was less pronounced. Their domain predominantly appeared to be upstairs. However, it was just the opposite case with the old woman. Lisa Ann felt her most strongly on this floor, specifically in a back bedroom. The feeling of sadness accompanying this spirit also felt stronger. As more information flowed in, a better picture of this sad old woman came into focus.

"I don't think she had children of her own," Lisa Ann said, and then thought, or more accurately, *listened* for another moment. "It's the children who cause all the commotion here, and she feels the need to watch over them."

Apparently, this old woman looked after the children when they were alive, and it is because of them that she is still connected to this house. In addition, in her final years she suffered ill health, and was

6

perhaps confined to a wheel chair. The emotional impact of that illness can still clearly be felt.

Our next stop was the basement. Lisa Ann's first impression was that homemade wine once filled racks along the walls. Other than that, she did not feel very much, even when she went into the small room that still contained the grave marker that seemed to spark trouble.

"I'm going to break protocol," I said, as I went back into the room to get the grave marker of the local woman. Handing the marker to Lisa Ann, I asked if any activity was connected to it.

To our surprise, she didn't feel as though this grave marker had anything to do with the spirits in the house. She "saw" a male relative of the deceased take the marker and bring it to the house, but no entity was attached to it.

"It's definitely not connected to the woman I feel in the house," she said. "The old woman I sense is from an earlier time, one of the first owners of the house."

She did sense something else in the basement, however; a male spirit, possibly that of a former handyman from that same early time period. While Cheryl still refuses to go into the basement alone because of the strong presence she feels, Lisa Ann did not see this man as sinister or threatening, although she felt he had been a heavy drinker. The most she would say about him was that he could be considered "creepy," and if Cheryl was sensitive to him than she had every right to be unnerved.

The next stop was the kitchen for a crucial part of the investigation—bagels and tea. As we ate, Lisa Ann summarized and clarified her findings.

"I think the old woman did live in the house, and she was one of the first owners. I don't think the kids ever lived here. I think she watched the kids or they used to like to play here, because they have a very fun, free-spirited energy about them, and they like to play.

"She (the old woman) has a sadness about her, and I'm still not understanding why she's so sad, but I do think she was in a wheelchair, or something like that, towards the end. Her energy is more downstairs, the kids are more upstairs.

"Outside by the stream it feels like someone had fallen, but didn't live here.

"In the basement is a man who took care of the house, maybe when the woman was older or sick.

"Nothing here is negative, and the kids don't realize they are scary. They run, move objects. She had money, the kids didn't. She spoiled them, gave them special food. They felt special being here, a safety zone."

After Lisa Ann's summary, we were finally able to let her know everything that had been happening, and how accurate she had been in sensing the nature of the paranormal activity in the house. Cheryl asked the names of the two children, and while Lisa Ann wasn't certain, she thought it might have been Mary and Michael. (Make note of this for later in the story!)

Lisa Ann asked if there was a farm up the street, as she felt that the children had walked to the house from a particular direction. Dan was able to confirm that some buildings in the area she described had been constructed on the site of an old farm. Again, she repeated that the old woman who cared for the two poor farm children never had kids of her own. She also felt that the children had died of illness around the same time, perhaps the victims of some local epidemic.

She also "saw" a script letter "E" as part of the woman's name, but admitted she had no sense whether it was a first or last name. It was odd that while the old woman did appear adamant about the "E," she did not provide a full name. I made a mental note to look for a script "E" on any material that might eventually be found someday.

I never imagined that day had already arrived.

After further discussion, it looked as though the investigation was over and we would be leaving shortly. But now it was my turn to hear a persistent voice in my head. I did not actually experience it as a distinct human voice, more of a feeling that the old woman did not want us to leave. In my mind I had the unmistakable message that there was more to be found, and we couldn't go until we found whatever was so important.

I didn't want to impose upon everyone as we had been there for several hours already, and everyone had things to do the rest of the day. Still, the feeling was strong, and if ten years of ghost hunting has taught me anything it's to go with your gut feeling—especially in a haunted location.

"Do you think if we went into Justin's room for a while with all the equipment we could get some evidence?" I suggested.

"No, they aren't in there now," Lisa Ann replied, then explained again how she felt that their presence would most likely only be able to be detected at night.

Still, that persistent urging would not take no for an answer, and I asked if anyone would mind trying anyway. Of course, Lisa Ann was right, and our cameras and instruments didn't pick up anything unusual. Still, there was more. I just knew there was something more.

Cheryl then told Lisa Ann about the night she witnessed the Victorian-style wedding gown floating in the living room. This led to the speculation that not only did the old woman not have children, but that she had never gotten married. (Only the empty gown had appeared to Cheryl, no one was wearing it.) Perhaps the woman had been engaged, and a tragedy or break-up had thwarted both her marital and maternal hopes.

"Is she here all the time?" I asked.

"Yes, but for some reason I get her up in the attic and I don't know why."

Dan explained that you can't stand upright in most sections of the attic, and again assured us that it was impossible to stand in front of the window where the old woman appeared, as the window was at floor level. (In other words, if someone was standing in front of that window, you would see their legs, not their face and torso.)

Why would this old woman appear to Lisa Ann in that window, and why would her presence be the strongest up there, when it was the main floors of the house where she lived and cared for the children?

I knew everyone was once again thinking the investigation was over, but I needed to get into that attic. I suggested we go up there for just a few minutes. I wanted to see that window, and see if there was any chance we could find some remnant of the past.

The stairs were incredibly narrow and steep, and there would have been no way an elderly and infirm woman would have been able to climb them. Dan had to move some boxes for us to all get up there, and then moved several more to give us space to squeeze through to different sections.

Lisa Ann did a bit of a balancing act by walking along beams out into a section that didn't have floorboards, but was rewarded by finding some newspapers from 1905, and a marvelous 1905 Macy's catalog which really gave a sense of the time with its fancy clothing, household items, jewelry, etc. (Including diamond rings for less than $10!)

I got on my hands and knees and crawled under a progressively lower slanted part of the attic in the back of the house. Poking around in the hundred-year-old dust I joked with Dan, "Is this your stack of hundred dollar bills back here?"

"Yeah, those are mine," he replied, "I wondered where I put them."

Of course, it would have been great to find a hidden stash of money, but in ghost investigator terms I was just about to find something priceless. I came upon on old photo of a woman on the beach (circa 1920s?), a piece of an old tortoise shell comb, an addressed envelope, and some bits and pieces of paper. Then way in the back I found a small, thin book covered in dust. At first I was disappointed that it appeared to be only an old school book, until I opened it.

Some of the items discovered in the attic.

The book was from 1902 and the owner had inscribed it Mary E. Drake—*emphasis on the fancy script "E."* Of course, this didn't mean it was the Mary in question (Cheryl always referred to the spirit as Mary, as she thought it was the woman from the grave marker. Perhaps she had been using the right name, but for the wrong reasons?) At the back of the book there were a couple of handwritten pages, but in the dim attic light they were hard to read.

We continued searching, and Lisa Ann felt that there was more to be discovered—under the floorboards near where I found the book. I wasn't about to push my luck and ask Dan to get a crowbar, but I was certainly tempted. We also checked out the window where the old woman had appeared, and indeed it was at floor level, so someone would have had to have been sitting or lying down to look out.

The attic window.

We brought our findings down to the kitchen and tried to decipher all the writing. Mike's detective skills helped, and an angled flashlight brought out more detail to some of the faint, penciled words.

He also pointed out how the pressure and style of the writing changed, suggesting that it had been written at different times, and under some emotional strain. I photographed everything, thinking that I might further enhance details on my computer later.

The two pages of handwritten notes in Mary E.'s book were indeed somewhat disjointed and rambling, and it was difficult to tell if she was writing to someone, or keeping a diary of sorts. There was a line about someone "being admitted to the bar," a paragraph about embroidering towels for some female friends, and curious emphasis on the line, "It had better be announced."

The real mind blowing sentence was to be discovered by Lisa Ann, as she slowly made out each word and read, "I ain't...got...nobody to...call me...mom..."

I don't think it would be an exaggeration to say that there were five completely stunned people in the room at that point. This was all too incredible! How many times had Lisa Ann repeated that this old woman had no children of her own? Why had I felt compelled to stay, and what were the chances that I would find a book in a remote corner of the attic that contained these words!

Talk about being stranger than fiction! I knew at that instant that this was one of my most remarkable cases ever. Just let a skeptic try to explain all this as mere coincidence.

The next day I enlarged and enhanced the photos of the writing in the book. I was still in a bit of a state of shock over the investigation, but I was even further amazed when I discovered the line, "I don't know any men," which would certainly lead one to believe that the writer was not married.

Of course, many questions remain. Who was Mary E. Drake, and was she the one who wrote those two pages in the back of the old school book? Who were the other people whose names we found on an envelope and a receipt? Could we ever track down the names and stories of the two children who still run through the halls playing?

Despite all of the many questions, we finally did have some remarkable answers. The families that now live in this house have seen and heard an old woman and a playful young boy and girl. Without any prior knowledge of the house, Lisa Ann immediately sensed the presence of a sad old woman and two energetic children. The woman regretted not ever having children, and we found a book in which a distraught woman wrote that she didn't have anyone "to call her mom."

One of the last things Lisa Ann said before we left that day was that she could still sense the presence of the woman, but that the feeling of sadness around her was no longer there. Perhaps she will begin to find real peace now that her story is coming to light after 100 years? It is clear now why she appeared in the attic window, so we would go up there and begin to unravel her past. Lisa Ann even speculated that perhaps this entire escalation of activity was not about the children, but a calculated attempt to cause enough of a disturbance so that we would return for the sake of the old woman.

More research will be needed, but just a few days after the investigation, Dan was able to find that the name on the envelope belonged to a family who owned the house in the early 1900s, and that the place was run as a boarding house during the 1910s. We will continue to search libraries, historic societies, and maybe even grab a couple of crowbars and start prying up floorboards in the attic.

As if this amazing story needed more startling events, a couple of nights after our visit, Cheryl noticed that a toy vacuum cleaner in Justin's room had been moved during the night. She asked Justin if he had moved it, and he replied, "No, I told Mike that he could play with it last night."

No one had told Justin what had occurred during the investigation, so he couldn't have had any idea that Lisa Ann had said she thought the children's names might be Michael and Mary. Throughout this entire ordeal, Justin had referred to the children as Jack and Jill, and now suddenly, out of the blue, he calls the boy Mike! My instincts tell me that the children were aware of what was happening, and wanted to give us one more affirmation that we were on the right track.

A few weeks later, I received some good news from Cheryl. She had switched her children's bedrooms, and both Justin and Aarron were able to sleep undisturbed. Shortly after, Justin explained that the kids would now be playing outside, and indeed activity in the house has effectively disappeared.

Is this the end of the story? Maybe, maybe not. It all depends upon the spirits, and whether or not they can now find peace after revealing vital information about their lives, and deaths.

I am still amazed by this case, and how so many pieces of the puzzle fit together. If I ever have doubts about what I do, I need only look back to this story to remind me that this is why I'm a ghost investigator.

# Suicide
## Orange County, NY

In 2005, Mike told me a fascinating story about a house in Orange County, New York, where a suicide had occurred, and subsequently, strange things happened to the family that bought the place. The details of the case were incredible, but early attempts to arrange a visit didn't pan out. Finally in October 2006, a chance meeting between Mike and the homeowner led to an investigation just a few days later.

Before delving into the story of this haunting, I want to say that this case represents both the best and the worst of what ghost hunting is all about. It is the best because the paranormal activity coincided with known events, with the primary entity actually being identified by name. It is the worst, because it involves terrible suffering and torment that has reached beyond the grave.

In August of 2004, "Jim and Alice" were about to buy a beautiful old farmhouse that had plenty of room for their two young boys. Right before the closing, they were told that the former owner had committed suicide in the house. It wasn't the best news, but as long as their boys knew nothing about it, they didn't see any problem with it. The suicide would be their secret—or so they had hoped.

Everything was fine for the first few months, then in December of 2004, their 4-year-old son, "Mark," came into the kitchen and said to Jim, "Daddy, there's a ghost in the house."

"Where?" Jim asked with little concern, thinking it was merely the boy's imagination.

"He's sitting right there," Mark replied, pointing to a chair in the corner of the dining room. Puzzled, he continued, "Don't you see him?"

"No, I don't see him. What does he want?"

"He wants you to sit on him," the boy said.

Thinking it was just a childish joke, Jim sat in the chair and his son burst out into "crazy laughter." Thinking the joke was over, Jim went back into the kitchen. A few minutes later his son returned.

"Dad, he's back."

"Well, what does he want?" Jim asked, continuing to play along with the odd game.

"He wants you to shoot him," he stated plainly.

14

The chair where Sam's spirit was first seen.

Jim's blood ran cold. The former owner had committed suicide by shooting himself. Why would his son say something like that? Was this some bizarre coincidence? He had to find out.

"What's his name?" Jim asked, fearful of the response.

"Sam," the boy said without hesitation.

That was it! The man who had shot himself to death in that house was named Sam! How could this be possible?

"Is he young or old?" Jim asked, knowing that Sam had been in his eighties.

"He's an old man."

Jim immediately called his wife at work.

"You won't believe what's going on!" he began, and then told her about what had just transpired. They were both stunned, and they hoped that this was only a one-time thing. Maybe now that Sam's restless spirit had made its presence known it would not appear again.

Unfortunately, that episode was not the end; it was only the beginning.

Shortly after this first incident, Mark said that Sam appeared at the foot of his bed one night, and he had a gun (a rifle or shotgun) on his back, and a large knife on his belt. While this was upsetting, it did provide more valuable evidence. Mark's bedroom had been Sam's bedroom, and the foot of Mark's bed corresponded to where Sam's bed had stood. Also, Sam was an avid hunter, so appearing with these weapons just reinforced the identity of the spirit.

The visits continued each night, until Mark became afraid to go into his bedroom. For four months he slept in his parents' room. During this time he began to see Sam on the television screen when it was turned off, and in the kitchen, sitting on the countertop in the corner.

As if the situation wasn't bad enough, a second, more ominous figure appeared. This one Mark called Batman, because he was all black and featureless. He would see Batman near the front door, but more often standing by a lamppost across the street. In fact, Mark would sit by the window and just stare for long periods of time. When questioned, he would say that he was looking at Batman, and couldn't understand why his parents couldn't see him, too.

Actually, one evening Jim did glimpse the dark figure. Through the three small windows in the front door, he saw a solid black figure that appeared to be looking in. In a moment, it was gone. Jim checked outside, but no one was in sight.

There was something odd about that front door. Soon after moving in, the family agreed to never ever use it, and always came and went through the back door. They also never sat on their front porch. There was just something uncomfortable about the front door and porch, and the best way to deal with that feeling was to completely avoid the main entrance to the house. It may not sound rational, but neither were the actions taken by the previous owner.

Sam had not only blacked out the windows in the door, he had actually boarded up the windows in the front of the house on the first floor! There is a very nice view from the front, so what would possess

16

someone to board them up? If it was a question of sunlight or privacy, why not use curtains and shades? And it could not have been a question of security, as there were many other windows on the first floor and in the basement that were left untouched. Perhaps this sinister figure appeared too often to Sam and his family?

Speaking of Sam's family, a distressing emotional encounter was soon to take place. Sam's daughter had heard through the grapevine about what Mark had been witnessing. Still traumatized by her father's suicide, she nonetheless needed to find out if the man she had known and loved was still in the house. Half of her hoped it was true and that she could make contact with him, while the other half was afraid her father's spirit was trapped.

One evening, she showed up at the door and said she had heard rumors about her father's ghost. She was clearly upset, but she needed to know if this was a reality, or a child's imagination. She was stunned by what she was about to hear.

Jim explained the first encounter Mark had with the man with the gun, and how he even knew the man's name. He said that Sam most often appeared in a chair in the corner of the dining room, and on a certain spot on the countertop in the kitchen. The daughter could barely believe what she was hearing.

It seems that for many years the family had big Sunday dinners at the house, and as is the case in most get-togethers, everyone always congregated in the kitchen. Her father's favorite place to be was sitting on the countertop in the corner, precisely where Mark always saw him. In addition, when everyone went in the dining room, Sam sat in his favorite chair in the corner by the front door, right where Mark first encountered the ghost who asked to be shot. (Sam's gun cabinet was also by that chair.)

It was all too much for the daughter and she quickly left in tears. It was a remarkable affirmation that added to the body of evidence, but it came at the steep price of mental and emotional anguish.

There continued to be occasional sightings, cold spots (particularly where the suicide occurred), and an inexplicable loud banging noise (as if something heavy hit the floor) on the second floor. Doors would sometimes slam, Jim always felt as if someone was watching him in the basement, and a friend who knew nothing about the house also "freaked out" in the basement because he, too, sensed a strong presence. Curiously, this presence only seems to affect men, as Alice never feels uncomfortable in the basement.

The basement.

One night when their niece was babysitting the two boys, they all clearly heard footsteps above them on the second floor. Thinking it must be an intruder, the niece bravely ran upstairs, but no one could be found. It's a night she will never forget.

One evening Jim heard Mark speaking loudly, as if arguing with someone. He naturally assumed that Mark was fighting with his older brother (who, by the way, rarely experienced anything unusual). After Mark shouted, "No, *you* shut up!" he decided he had better go see what the boys were fighting about. When Jim entered the room, he found that Mark was all alone.

"Who were you talking to?" he asked.

"Sam told me to shut up, so I told him to shut up, and I'm mad at him!" the boy replied as if he had just had a perfectly normal argument with a real person.

The angry paranormal encounter had a curious effect. Whether Sam was offended or Mark chose to shut down the lines of communication, things became quiet. For a period of about 6 to 8 months there wasn't any unusual activity. Then the date for our investigation was set...

A couple of days before we arrived, Jim and Alice were in an outbuilding on their property that they had converted into a game room and bar. Some friends were there, and as Jim was telling them that I would be investigating the haunted activity, a large sign came off the wall and hit the bar.

"It didn't fall, it was *launched*!" Jim exclaimed when he showed me the sign and where it landed.

At the time, they tried to find a natural explanation, such as something or someone striking the outside wall, but there's a locked storage area on the other side, so no tree limbs or people could have made contact. They also explained that the sign's hanger, which was one of those deep, saw-toothed hangers, sat firmly on a secure screw in the wall. The sign had to be lifted up before it could move forward, and would take considerable force to have it land several feet from the wall.

This was clearly a belligerent act, uncharacteristic of the generally benign appearances that Sam had made. In addition, Sam had never been spotted outside of the house, and spirits connected to a particular site rarely seem to have the will or ability to wander.

No, everything pointed to something else; something darker that roamed the property. Perhaps Batman was not happy at the prospect of ghost hunters prying into his domain?

When we first arrived that evening, Jim and Alice gave us a rundown on everything that occurred since they moved in. We examined the game room and sign, and found that it indeed would have required a force to lift it up and out. In other words, it was no accident.

19

The sign that came off the wall (see arrow). Jim's hand indicates where the sign landed on the bar, several feet from the wall.

Then Bob, Mike, and I were left alone in the house to begin the investigation. It was business as usual as we set up cameras and instruments, and no one felt particularly tense. That may sound odd, but after a few dozen murder and suicide-related hauntings, you kind of get used to it. I mention this because it's important to know our mental states. I was curious, but not apprehensive. There was anticipation, but no fear. Like I said, it was business as usual—but when that business is ghost hunting, the situation can change in one awful heartbeat...

As Bob and Mike were setting up a camcorder and EMF meter on the second floor, I was at the bottom of the stairs setting up another camcorder. As we worked, I heard the back door open, and I assumed that it was Jim or Alice. I waited a moment, but didn't hear any footsteps. When no one spoke, I said, "Hello?" No one responded, and I didn't hear the door close, so I went into the kitchen (I had only been a few feet from the kitchen).

To my complete surprise, the kitchen was empty. Even stranger, the door was not only closed tight, but Mike had secured the chain lock (which I didn't know), so no one could possibly have opened the door! Bob and Mike hadn't heard anything upstairs, but I have no doubt that I heard the sound of that door opening.

After everything was up and running, we went down into the basement. As we stood quietly in the dark, we heard a loud bang or thud from somewhere upstairs. However, even though we had camcorders running on both floors, the sound was not recorded, which didn't make any sense—from a normal perspective, that is.

What also didn't make "normal" sense is what neighbors had observed when the house was vacant for some time after the suicide. They would see the basement light go on, and after a while it would turn off. They checked to see if all the doors and windows were secure, and there were no signs of a break in. Failing any rational explanations, they chalked it up to Sam.

No lights went on when we were in the basement, and none of us saw or felt anything unusual after the banging sound, so we moved upstairs. However, unbeknownst to us at the time, the camcorder in the kitchen—which was aimed at Sam's corner—did record something we had never seen before.

It took a couple of weeks to go through all of the video footage from that night. As I was watching the footage of the kitchen, I suddenly saw a dark object several inches long streak across the field of view. Startled, I quickly rewound the tape to see if my eyes were playing tricks on me, but there it was again.

21

Over the years, we've recorded all kinds of moths, bugs, and dust moving through the air—all of which reflect the IR (infrared) light and appear bright white. However, this object was totally black. As it moved very quickly (less than half a second to go approximately 10 feet), it was definitely not dust, and it didn't move like an insect, either. It appeared to originate from the window (which was closed) or the wall right in front of where Sam used to sit, and moved out and up at an angle until it exited the camcorder's field of view—and it did so in the blink of an eye. In addition, the EMF meter alarm was sounding.

When I sent the video clip to Mike, he was equally puzzled. He observed that if it had been the shadow of an object moving behind the camcorder, there would have to have been a light source, which there was not. It did appear to be a solid object actually moving through the air. By why did it appear so black?

I called Jim that night and asked if he had any clue what it could be. He confirmed that they had never seen any large bugs in the house, especially ones that flew quickly. It remains a mystery to this day.

A frame from the infrared camcorder footage. The black spot can be seen by the edge of the refrigerator (see arrow), and the long line illustrates the path the spot moved along. It may not look like much in this picture, but the video is startling. The EMF meter is on the counter where Sam used to sit.

We decided to sit quietly at the base of the stairs by the front door and see if anything happened. Nothing at all happened for quite some time, and finally Mike said, "We are going to leave if you don't give us a sign—anything to let us know you're here. If you can hear us, come to the top of the stairs."

Less than a minute later, the EMF meter at the top of the stairs went off! Personally, I got goose bumps and it suddenly felt icy cold. Could this be Sam making an appearance? Mike went upstairs and sat in the hallway off to the side near the bedrooms. Shortly after, he heard footsteps and saw something moving in the shadows, and then it was gone. Bob and I did not hear anything from where we sat at the bottom of the stairs, which only meant one thing—activity was increasing upstairs, so that's where I had to go.

My next decision will literally haunt me the rest of my life. I decided to sit on the suicide spot. The spot where a desperate old man had taken his life while his family sat on the back porch and listened in horror to the fatal gunshot. The spot where the new owners, Jim and Alice, decided to tear up the carpeting over a year later and found that Sam's blood still stained the floor. The spot where a tormented soul should have found release, but instead remains trapped between the worlds of the living and the dead.

It was not one of my smartest moves...

We sat for several minutes asking questions, trying to elicit some kind of response. I didn't really have any unusual sensations at first, and began to think nothing would come of this unorthodox experiment. Then a sudden chill swept through me, and I felt as if my mind was being pulled toward images and thoughts that weren't my own. Over and over I began hearing the first line of an old Christian hymn, "What a friend we have in Jesus, all our sins and griefs to bear..."

Now, I am probably the least *religious* person I know, so it wasn't something that was coming from me. (I try to adhere to a *spiritual* life. I see distinct differences between religion and spirituality. As past and recent history has proven time and again, because you wear the clothes of a clergyman, or go to a church, temple, etc. on a regular basis, it doesn't mean you are a spiritual person. Just check the headlines every day to see what "religious" people are doing to hurt innocent men, women, and children.)

So there I was, sitting on the suicide site, and these words and music are playing over and over in my head like a broken record. I told Bob and Mike what was happening, and Mike asked, "Sam, are you trying to tell us that you were religious?"

23

As he spoke those words, my heart seemed to break and tears began to flow.

"You all right?" Mike whispered.

"No," was all I could manage in reply.

"Do you want to go downstairs?" he asked.

It would probably have been the wise thing to do, but I was so wrapped up in emotions I had to ride it out.

"*He* absolutely knew it was wrong..." I said, carefully choosing my words, as I was inclined to say "I" instead of "He" because it felt so real, so personal. "...so against what he believed, but he felt so bad he couldn't take it anymore."

It is difficult to describe how awful I felt, and how overwhelmed with a terrible sadness, guilt, and remorse. Even many months later, it is still difficult to watch the video of me sitting on the floor in tears, as it brings it all back with painful clarity.

Then, just like the flick of a switch, it was gone. One second I was in anguish and not in control of my thoughts and emotions, the next second I was myself again—with "myself" probably being the keyword here. Whoever it was had gotten his message across and had left. I had asked for it, and I had gotten it, big time.

Mike asked again if I wanted to take a break. Even though I claimed to be okay, Bob also strongly suggested it was time to step away from the suicide site. I relented, but when I went to stand up I found I was a bit shaky. Mike helped me to my feet, and Bob helped me down the stairs—my one hand on his shoulder, my other gripping the railing. I thought the episode was over, but the really scary part was just seconds away.

As we all got downstairs, I let go of Bob and everything in my head seemed to swirl and fade. I believe I had just enough time to exclaim, "Whoa!" before hitting the floor. I didn't fall forward or back, just sunk straight down as every muscle had just gone limp.

"Are you all right? What happened?" Bob asked with concern as he reached down to help me up.

"I...fell over," came my brilliant response, and then I told him to give me a minute before I tested my legs again.

"Were you pushed?" Mike asked.

"No, just woozy...couldn't stand up straight," I replied.

Mike was particularly concerned because of what he had witnessed just an instant before I dropped. Through the windows of the front door (which was just a few feet away from us) he saw a dark figure peering inside. The figure seemed to realize that it had been seen, then turned and took off. Before Mike had time to speak, I hit the floor.

That was all I needed to hear in my condition.

"I need to get out of this," I said. To this day I'm not sure why I said *this* instead of *here*. "I'm a wreck."

As soon as I finished speaking, the EMF meter at the top of the stairs began wailing again, as if confirm that things had gotten out of hand and it really was time to go.

Had this black figure been drawn to the house again because of the emotions that had been stirred up, because it somehow feeds on those awful feelings? Had that figure somehow caused me to fall by drawing away my energy? Of course, I can't say for certain, but I don't think the events in the house and the appearance of the figure at the door where a coincidence. I also believe from all that had gone on that the dark figure seeks out negative emotions, and can exacerbate bad situations.

As we packed up, we told Jim and Alice what had transpired. I think it's always a mixed reaction to our reported findings—on the one hand, homeowners are relieved to hear that they aren't the only ones experiencing weird things, while on the other hand, they have to face the fact that what's been happening is not just their imagination, that they are living with ghosts. In this case, I think the homeowners are coping remarkably well, but unfortunately—and understandably—that isn't always the case.

Speaking of coping, I wasn't exactly in the best shape after leaving that night. I recall thinking two things on the way home. First, it was a good thing I wasn't driving. Second, I hoped that the impact of the "close encounter" wasn't going to have any lasting effects. In the short term, say a day or two, I was still very upset by the whole experience. As time passed, those initial intense feelings faded, but even now there is that lingering twinge when I recollect that night's ordeal. And it all came flooding back the next time I went to the house.

It was several months later when psychic Lisa Ann was checking out Mike's grandmother's house (written about in several past books). Since Jim and Alice's house was just a short drive from there, she was kind enough to agree to stop by. We knew that no one would be home, but we were curious to see what she would sense from the property— something of a "drive-by reading," but you make the best of all opportunities.

As usual, we didn't tell Lisa Ann anything about the property or the activity, so the first thing she knew was when Mike stopped the car on the street in front of the house and said that this was the place.

Her first reaction was that there is a "grayness" along the entire street, not just this house and yard. I know Mike had previously stated that he felt there was something odd about this area, as well, and he had recounted its violent past when Indians had conducted bloody raids along this very road in colonial times.

Next she sensed an entity, not from inside the house, but on the property—the front yard and porch, in particular! Mike and I were all ears as we felt the excitement that can only come from these extraordinary validations. Continuing, Lisa Ann described the entity as a very angry, negative male, and she went so far as to use the term evil to describe him.

Without revealing what we knew about the dark figure on the porch, we asked a few questions to see if we could find some clues as to this man's identity and motives. She felt that he was from the late 1800s, and his anger stemmed from something to do with his wife leaving him, although the circumstances surrounding her leaving were hazy. Had she run off with another man? Had she left without telling him anything? Had she faked her own death to escape him? Whatever had taken place over a hundred years ago, this spirit had yet to deal with the situation and was seeking some kind of knowledge and closure regarding his wife.

In the meantime, he would make other people's lives miserable. Lisa Ann felt that he was attracted to negative emotions, perhaps even feeding off the darker energies of depression and anger that might be generated by anyone living in the house.

Now didn't that all sound familiar! As usual, she was batting a thousand, but what she said next surprised us.

She began describing another man, someone who had been desperate, and had committed suicide, most likely by shooting himself. Naturally, we assumed she was speaking about Sam, but she went on to describe a young man, distraught over some work-related issue, who had killed himself outside, back in the trees behind the small game room building. Lisa Ann specifically stated that this man had "his whole life ahead of him," and perhaps he had some sort of chemical imbalance or clinical depression that contributed to his desperate act.

A young suicide victim? A man who had shot himself out in the yard, not in the house? Could the psychic signals have been getting crossed, or had there been an earlier suicide at this location? It was not something we had anticipated, but was now clearly something we had to consider, especially after the additional information Lisa Ann was about to divulge.

While Mike and I pondered the startling new information, Lisa Ann pointed to the second floor of the house and said she sensed another spirit. This description did fit Sam, and when she seemed to hesitate describing yet another man who had shot himself, I finally spoke up and said that she was on the right track. And something else began to happen during her description—I started to cry.

As she was telling us about the other two entities, I was fascinated, but detached. However, as soon as she tuned into Sam, I felt my emotions rising to the point where the feelings from that painful night of the investigation all resurfaced. While this is hardly verifiable scientific proof, to my mind this was a validation that Lisa Ann had connected with Sam's energy, and that there were then at least three separate and distinct spirits at this location.

As upset as I was, I still continued to ask questions, and Lisa Ann sensed that Sam wasn't really trapped at this location, it was more the fact that he loved this house and liked being there. However, she did sense that the negative entity may have affected him when he was alive, and could possibly still have some influence on him even now.

The atmosphere was tense and somber in the car as we sat outside this suicide house, but things eased considerably at the most unexpected moment. I mentioned to Lisa Ann how I had chosen to sit on the spot where Sam had killed himself, and without missing a beat she asked, "And how did that work for you?"

Enough said. Fools do rush in…

The bottom line is this—Sam is there, and while his presence can be unnerving and upsetting to the people in the house, it is not threatening. There is most likely another suicide victim from an earlier time, who is also unsettling but not dangerous. Then there is the dark entity on the porch and yard. Lisa Ann believes that he is capable of affecting the family, and that no one prone to depression should live there, as this entity will make bad situations worse.

As remarkable as this story was to this point, there were still some surprises in store. Several months later, Mike called to tell me that one of Jim's co-workers, who also lived on the same street, had a similar situation—his grandfather had shot himself to death in the house and people were seeing and feeling a male presence (see story, page 108).

27

What are the chances of two such cases on the same street! Perhaps what Lisa Ann said about a "grayness" over the entire area is related to either the cause or effect of these tragedies.

The other bizarre occurrence happened to Mike about eight months after our investigation. One day out of the blue, a woman he had worked with for many years came up to him and announced that she was Sam's granddaughter! She had heard about the story and read about Mike on my website, and was eager to find out what we knew, as well as share what she knew about the family and house. This was either some incredible coincidence, or just another weird twist of fate. In my experience, I would have to tend to believe the latter.

I'll never forget when Mike called and asked if I was sitting down, and then told me that Sam's granddaughter, "Beth", wanted to speak with me and would be able to fill in many of the missing pieces. Minutes later I was speaking with her and getting some very valuable firsthand information on the case. (I do want to point out that I could have tracked down Sam's relatives and asked them questions, but these are very sensitive situations—especially where suicides are involved—and I never feel it's appropriate to dredge up painful emotions for the sake of a story. So, when a relative comes to me willing to talk, it is a great privilege and opportunity.)

One of the first surprising pieces of information was that Beth was not at all surprised that Sam was still there in spirit. He loved the house and property, and always felt like no one could take care of it like he could. Beth said that the place was the hub of all family activities—including her own wedding—and that when Sam died, his ashes were spread across the property.

She was also able to correct a crucial misconception. It had been thought that Sam had brain cancer and possibly was not in his right mind when he killed himself. In fact, it was colon cancer, and Beth said his mind was clear until the day he died. And what she said next was startling at first, but then made a lot of sense.

"His suicide was the most unselfish act I ever saw," Beth stated, with touching emotion in her voice.

She went on to explain that Sam had grown increasing dependent on others, and hated the idea of being a burden on his wife and family. Yes, he was in pain, but it was love that motivated him to end his life.

However, as noble as this may sound, his suicide truly resulted in multiple tragedies. In addition to his death, there was the awful grief of the family members that heard the shot and were horrified at his sudden, violent death. Even worse, Sam's own daughter witnessed the shooting!

The family had just finished one of their big Sunday dinners, and everyone went out onto the back porch. Shortly after, Sam's daughter came back into the house for something, and saw Sam carrying a gun toward the staircase. She implored her father to put down the gun as he climbed the stairs, but he yelled at her to go away, and insisted that he had to do this. When he reached the top of the stairs, he pulled the trigger and died right before her eyes. Clearly, he had not intended for anyone to see this, and perhaps some of the residual guilt is from subjecting his daughter to such an awful sight.

Beth told me that her grandmother had also died in the house, of natural causes. Family members grew concerned when she wasn't answering her phone, and went to the house to find that she had passed away in a chair in the living room near the front door. (The proximity of the place of her passing to the front door does concern me in lieu of the dark figure.)

Finally, we spoke about any prior paranormal activity, and if Beth had ever experienced the dark figure. While she had never personally encountered anything unusual, several relatives had told her that there had always been "spirit activity" there. That's all they said, so she has no way of knowing just how many spirits or what kind of activity there was, but it did sound as if things had been happening for many decades, at least.

As for past history of occupants and possible tragedies, Beth knew nothing. However, she does plan to ask some relatives what they might know about former owners and personal experiences. The most important issues, however, remain the states of the three spirits here—the two suicide victims who need release, and the evil dark presence that needs to be stopped. And let us not forget the living who must now deal with all this past anguish that has tainted the house and property. We can only hope and pray that more victims are not added to the list of those that suffer here.

# The Shanley Hotel
## Napanoch, NY

When you're headed to a haunted place, there's nothing like a good thunderstorm to put you in the mood. Of course, one wouldn't typically expect a thunderstorm on December 1, but the weather had been unusually warm, and a powerful cold front was sweeping in from the Midwest. When the two met, sparks were flying—in the form of deadly lightning bolts.

As Mike and I headed north on Route 17 in Orange County, New York, the storm hit with its full fury. The fierce wind-driven rain made it almost impossible to see, so we got off at the nearest exit and waited it out. Once it was safe to continue we got back on the road, but the damage had been done. Sadly, we passed a house on Route 209 where a huge tree had just fallen and killed the occupant.

Nothing like a dark and stormy night of death and destruction to set the mood.

Downtown Napanoch, such as it is, is something of a step back in time, and Shanley's Hotel is the impressive showpiece of this once bustling tourist area. We were surprised at how large it was—three stories with a spacious porch. It must have been magnificent in its prime, and will no doubt be another gem once fully restored.

The first hotel on the site was the Hotel Napanoch built in 1845. It was a smaller structure, and it burned down in March of 1895. Just six months later, they were already plastering the walls of the new, larger hotel. Thanks to the railroad, tourists from New York City came to Napanoch to enjoy the beautiful mountain scenery. While some of the wealthiest tourists stayed at the exclusive Yama Farms Inn, the men would still come to the Hotel Napanoch in the evenings as it had something their fancier counterpart did not—a bar!

Something of a Who's Who of celebrities and notable people passed through the doors of the hotel in the late 19th and early 20th centuries, but it was to also have a less reputable history. In 1905, James Shanley bought the hotel. His family owned several restaurants in New York City, and while the establishment continued to thrive under his experienced management, he also began some shadier enterprises.

In 1932, Shanley's Hotel was raided by federal marshals on two occasions, as Mr. Shanley was running a bootlegging operation (dealing in illegal liquor during Prohibition). An addition was also built in 1910 to the back of the bar area, and this structure reputedly became a brothel. Of course, such a business would not be listed with the Better Business Bureau so there is no documented evidence that has yet come to light, but many local residents have confirmed that this oldest of professions was practiced at Shanley's until very late in the 20th century.

Mr. Shanley died in the mid-1930s, and as none of his three children lived beyond six months, the hotel passed into the hands of other owners. The glory days were over in its final decades, and the place shut down in 1992. It remained vacant and crumbling until Sal and Cindy Nicosia purchased the property in 2005.

We were greeted by Barbara Bleitzhofer, a psychic who had acquainted me with the fascinating story of Shanley's Hotel. She told me dozens of stories about the place, and I remember thinking that if even half of them were true this would be one of my most remarkable investigations. I admit, I never thought that all the stories put together would only be a small part of the tangled mass of paranormal activity that engulfs the living in every room, corridor and staircase.

First impressions are always very telling, and my immediate reaction upon entering the building told me volumes—and they weren't happy bedtime stories. As my attention was drawn up the main staircase, I pulled back emotionally as I felt as if something terrible had occurred there. I later found out that a woman had fallen to her death on those stairs. It was a potent psychic, psychological, and emotional reaction, and I had barely gotten both feet in the door!

Mike on the staircase, looking down to the front door.

*If the rest of the hotel is anything like this,* I thought...

I managed to take several more steps without any further encounters, and Barbara introduced us to the owners, Sal and Cindy, who have undertaken the tremendous task of restoring the structure with plans to once again open it to the public as a bed and breakfast. We sat in the large open room on the first floor that used to be the bar, and over tea, coffee, cookies, and pastries, I took notes on the history of the place and everyone's experiences.

When I asked them about their first paranormal experience in the building they all chuckled, as if to say, "Where should we start?" It was obviously difficult to say what came first—the footsteps, voices, shadowy figures or the feelings of a strong presence.

One night soon after Sal and Cindy moved into their second floor rooms, they heard very loud footsteps coming up the staircase from the first floor. Their initial thoughts did not involve ghosts as the footsteps sounded so real. They thought that perhaps someone in town had seen lights on in the hotel, and not realizing the long-derelict structure was once again occupied, had called the police.

However, when they went to see if a cop was on their staircase, they found no one. Sal searched the rest of the house and found that all of the doors and windows were securely locked, and no other living person was in the old hotel.

Much of activity takes place in the former bar area. One night they placed a baby monitor in the large room, then sat upstairs and listened. Very shortly afterward they heard voices and movement, as if the bar was back in operation. Again thinking it was living intruders, Sal came downstairs and unlocked the door to the bar. The moment he stepped inside the sounds abruptly stopped. However, as soon as he closed and locked the door again, the sounds of voices and activity began. Cindy then came downstairs and told the spirits to "knock it off," and finally there was peace and quiet.

Then there are the odd phenomena of the "balancing acts," as they call them. Their grandson tossed his toy penguin to the floor, and it landed on its head and stayed perfectly upright and motionless as if being held in place. As this toy penguin was just as bottom heavy as the living varieties, everyone was amazed to see this lopsided toy perfectly balanced upside down. Ever since then they have tried to make the penguin stand on its head, with absolutely no success.

Another incident involved a hired worker who was in the back of the bar area near the door to the outside (which incidentally still had the small sliding panel in it from the bootlegging days). The door was open, and he turned for a moment to get some tools. When he turned back, there was a chestnut balanced on top of the door. At first glance this doesn't seem particularly paranormal as a nut could have fallen and landed in just the right way. However, he took down the chestnut, then repeatedly tried to balance it on the edge of the door again, but found it was impossible due to the size and shape of both the nut and the top edge of the door.

Truly a unique way of getting someone's attention! So why the balancing acts? Of course it's all speculation, but there does seem to be questions of balance throughout Shanley's—or more accurately lack of balance; but more on that later.

33

There are also many cold spots, as well as the more rare hot spots. The smell of cigar smoke often hangs in the air, although no one smokes cigars. Clothes and hair have been tugged, there have been several incidents of being pushed (which was more like being pushed out of the way rather than being attacked), radio dials spin, doors open and sometimes the atmosphere is so oppressive it's difficult to breathe. There was also the sound of a clock chiming the hour, when there were not yet any clocks in the building.

They discovered that two women who lived alone in the place in the recent past experienced much of the same paranormal activity, including phantom piano music, which didn't cease even after they removed the piano. At first they thought that people were breaking in, so they waited by the door one night with baseball bats. When they realized the sounds were being generated by things *inside* the building they quickly moved out.

In the late 1980s, a regular patron of the bar went into the bathroom, and as he stood there relieving himself, he had the oddest sensation that someone was watching him. The feeling grew very intense, and when he spun around to see who had dared to disturb him at such a moment, he came face to face with a stern looking woman in a Victorian-era dress. The man ran terrified from the bathroom and refused to ever step back in there. However, his fear didn't prevent him from returning to the bar on a regular basis. It was just that from that day, whenever nature called he would go home to use his own bathroom, then return to the bar!

When I asked how many spirits they thought inhabited Shanley's, Sal and Barbara both agreed that there seemed to be about nine to eleven distinct entities, with two or three being children, several women, and a couple of men. I was taking notes as they spoke, and I repeated their words of "nine to eleven." As I said "eleven," the lights in the room suddenly brightened, as if I had the right answer. Sal said the electricity in this section was all brand new and without problems, so we couldn't blame the wiring for the inexplicable brightening!

I then asked if there had been any murders, suicides or other deaths in the hotel over of the years, and Sal replied that there had been "quite a few." It is common for an establishment of this type and age to have its share of deaths, but Shanley's seems to have more than its share, and more of the violent variety.

We certainly now had a good background on the place and were anxious to get started on the investigation. We first took a tour of all the floors and basement in what should have been an opportunity for us to orient ourselves with the layout of the many rooms. Instead, Mike and I both became disoriented and somewhat dazed. Looking back, it reminds me of one of those scenes from a movie where someone has to pass between lines of people beating him—running the gauntlet, they call it. Well, Mike and I ran the extrasensory gauntlet and were definitely psychically bruised as a result. And that was just the beginning.

The staircase and landings can present an eerie picture in the darkness of the old hotel.

The first stop on our tour was the coat closet—not a location typically associated with haunted activity, but this was no ordinary closet. There was a hidden panel in the floor that led to a secret basement room. It was in this room that Mr. Shanley held meetings regarding his illegal bootlegging operations during Prohibition. If you saw Mr. Shanley's hat hanging on a peg above the closet, it meant he was down in the room and was not to be disturbed. Mike and I decided when we set up our equipment, that secret room would be one of the locations.

We didn't go into the room right then; we wanted to continue our walkthrough and get the full picture of the place. The next stop was the original kitchen/dining area. A psychic, who did not know that this was once a kitchen, sensed a lot of movement here, and "saw" things being passed through a wall. Of course, that didn't seem to make sense, until it was learned that in the early days all of the cooking was done in a building in the back of the property, and the cooked food was passed through a window that was once in that wall.

As we ascended the main staircase, there were strong EMF readings about half the way up. Mike and I agreed this was a "tense area," and it was at this point that we learned a woman had fallen to her death here. It is a palpable residue that remains from this tragedy.

As the atmosphere was already very heavy, it was a very pleasant surprise to find a few bedrooms on the second floor that had already been fully restored and decorated. Cindy has done an amazing job of hand-stenciling the floors, wallpapering, and adding just the right combinations of fabrics and colors. The cozy Victorian bedrooms almost made us forget that we were in a very haunted place. However, in one of the bedrooms the high EMF readings, feeling of a female presence, and chills up our spines quickly reminded us.

Next we went to the apartment rooms that were occupied by Sal and Cindy, and their dog and cat who often act strange for no visible reason. They feel that Mr. Shanley still resides here, and a rocking chair that rocks on its own is further evidence that they are not alone. There is also a gentle female presence that inhabits the former sun porch, now enclosed. They all believe this to be the spirit of a woman named Esther who was Mr. Shanley's sister-in-law, who died in childbirth.

Esther's husband had not treated her well, and was only interested in having her give him a son. After she died (along with the baby boy to whom she had just given birth), her husband took off and never returned, abandoning his daughters, whom Mr. Shanley then raised.

This sad spirit of the once beautiful woman often makes her presence known here, but never in a threatening or frightening manner.

A second floor bedroom where we got high EMF readings. (Infrared image.)

The third floor was something of a challenge—emotionally as well as physically. There was no electricity, as no restoration had yet taken place here, and floorboards were missing in many rooms. There was also plastic covering the windows, and with the strong winds still howling from the storm, the rippling and banging sounds from the blowing plastic kept you on your toes (as if we needed anything else to keep our senses on high alert).

The staircase leading up to the third floor is one of the areas where they see and feel the "Piano Man." Several decades ago, an elderly and poor man who lived in the hotel used to play the piano to earn a few tips in the bar. Despite being essentially destitute, he always dressed in a very dapper manner, and his ghost still appears well-dressed and groomed. He also continues to play the piano, as several people have heard music, although until recently there wasn't even a piano in the place!

Many residents of Napanoch remember the Piano Man, but no one could remember his name—until a couple of weeks after our visit, when someone in town recalled that his name was Sam. Unfortunately, Sam was buried in a pauper's grave, and there may not be any marker or records to give any more information on his life. In any event, such information may not be necessary, as we know where he is now…

On the third floor, Barbara pointed to a room across the hall to our left where they have heard and recorded what sounds like someone using a typewriter. It seems many of the ghosts are sticking to what they did in life.

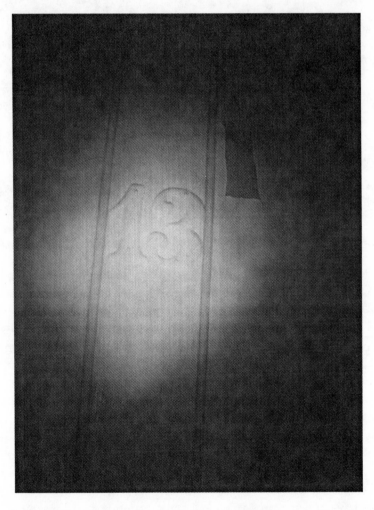

Room #13, or was it? Curiously, the numbers were not in any order, and it is suspected that when a tragedy occurred in a room its number was quickly changed.

The first room we entered to our right at the other end of the building was extremely disorienting. Later, I was able to compare it with what I would imagine it would be like stepping into an alternate reality, but when I was in the moment I could only feel confused and somewhat agitated. A visiting psychic had recorded a very loud, "NO!" in response to one of his questions in this room.

Several times on this floor, I thought I heard a few seconds of music, and there were instances of strong emotions that passed as quickly as they came. Fleeting EMF readings were measured here and there, but nothing consistent.

I commented that everything was happening "in little snippets," and that "there were brief glimpses being shot at you" in rapid succession. Many haunted locations involve a couple of spirits with fairly set patterns of behavior, in fairly localized places. This was very unusual—many, many spirits, the full gamut of emotions, different experiences with every step, almost nothing sustained, everything cutting deep psychically. I realized I had never been in such a place before and I wasn't sure I liked it. In fact, I knew I didn't. Yet, it was fascinating!

As I struggled with my own disorienting feelings, I looked over at Mike who had a knitted brow and a far off expression. I asked him if he was all right, and although he appeared very distracted, he said he was okay to continue. Concerned, I kept an eye on him, and shortly after I saw this odd look on his face as he was muttering something, as if having a conversation with someone.

"Mike, what's the matter?" I asked, never having seen him like this before in all of our investigations. "What are you saying?"

He looked at me as if from another world and said he was fine, and wasn't saying anything. When I told him he had just been speaking, he had no recollection of it. This was getting really scary now. Of all the tense and frightening situations we had been in over the years, this was the first time I had seen him like this. As dazed and disoriented as I was, Mike was clearly in another world—which can be a very dangerous thing.

I suggested taking a break to clear his head, but he assured me again that he was okay, so we continued.

In the next room, I had the immediate impression of a child, and for some reason found myself looking up at the ceiling. Barbara was somewhat pleased by my reaction, as she also senses a child in this room, and also feels compelled to look up. She felt that perhaps there was once a mobile hanging from the ceiling at which the child used to look up at for hours on end.

The next room was even more unnerving, as the sense of sadness, loss, and death hung in the air. Barbara explained that one day when she was in this room she put her hand against the wall and suddenly "heard" a woman's voice calling out a man's name. It was the plaintive cry of a woman who had lost her love. When Barbara asked what had happened, the woman became angry and said another man had been responsible for her loss, and named that man, as well.

Remarkably, when Barbara was relating this story to a friend, the woman recognized the names of the two men. With a little digging, a tragic story emerged. A man who lived next to Shanley's Hotel was in love with a prostitute who lived there, and it was his name spoken so lovingly by the spirit. The name that had been spoken angrily was that of his best friend, who warned the man against getting emotionally involved with a prostitute and insisted the relationship must be ended.

Soon after, the prostitute died in the hotel of an "accident" at the hands of one of the men. However, some local residents believe it was murder and that it had been covered up. And the reason I have not divulged the names of the two men involved is that they are still living today. If this is all just rumor and hearsay, I'm not about to accuse two innocent men of murder, and many local residents of a cover-up. However, if there *is* truth to this story, then it is no wonder that this distraught spirit still haunts this room, while the guilty men responsible for her death are living full lives.

As we all stood in the room where the woman had died and listened to Barbara relate the sad story, there was suddenly the most bone-chilling moaning sound. Common sense told us it must be the wind, but the hair standing up on top of our goose bumps made us feel that there was something else behind it. It was classic horror movie soundtrack moaning, but the wind can play tricks in old drafty houses.

Another psychic had also sensed the spirit of a murdered woman in this room. In fact, he also "heard" a sound like that of a neck being broken, which is apparently how the prostitute died. With so much evidence and experiences from different sources it would be hard to label this all a coincidence, despite what local residents say.

An interesting note about what local residents say—or more importantly, don't say—about Shanley's Hotel: Several people have said that their grandparents used to tell them to avoid the place. Even today, Barbara, Sal, and Cindy are amused when they watch people walking down the sidewalk, who then cross the street before reaching the hotel, then cross back once they have passed the property line, so that they are never close to the building!

Other "Oldtimers" are very reluctant to speak of the hotel's checkered past. They will often whisper, "There are things I could tell you about that place," and then will "clam up" and refuse to give any details. There is a considerable amount of fear and reluctance to speak, as well as a healthy dose of denial.

Recently, when Barbara was asking someone in town some general history questions about the history of the hotel, the woman blurted out, "And there aren't ANY ghosts there!" An interesting comment, considering that wasn't even one of the questions!

One last experience of note occurred on the third floor during the walkthrough. In one spot Barbara and Cindy felt "woozy" and their legs were heavy and weak. There was a distinct whisper from one of the hallways, and a chill went up my spine. While the two men were unaffected, we three women had definite and strong sensations—as I described it at the time, I was "having center of gravity difficultly." Unfortunately, this would not be the last or strongest sensation of having trouble standing.

After the somewhat traumatic third floor, came one of the most intense areas at Shanley's—the brothel. Conveniently located adjacent to the bar, the brothel rooms are accessed through a doorway and up some steep and narrow stairs. There is a small alcove at the top of the stairs, where an old woman used to sit, keeping an eye on everyone entering and exiting.

There are three bedrooms, a storage area, and an opening leading to a large attic space. Again, no restoration has taken place in this area, and there aren't any lights or electricity. But there is certainly plenty of "atmosphere," of the paranormal variety, and none of it is too pleasant.

In one room I felt completely off-balance and commented that, "I feel like I want to fall backwards." I bent down to check the floorboards and they were level and solid. So why did it feel like the floor was moving and shifting under my feet? The sensation was something like those carnival funhouses that have floors that spin and move up and down—only this wasn't much fun!

"I have to get out of here," I said as I quickly left the room, fortunately regaining my stability as soon as I went into another room.

41

"At least I don't feel like I'm going to fall over in here," I said with some relief.

Apparently, this sensation is nothing new at Shanley's, as several people have ended up falling or being pushed down. I did not intend on being one of them—but ghost investigators can't be choosers, as I was to later discover, much to my chagrin.

Suddenly we all heard footsteps from somewhere in the brothel, and we were quickly able to confirm that none of us had generated the sounds. Mike then felt compelled to open the storage area door—which had yet to be opened since they bought the place—and when he did, Cindy smelled a foul odor rushing out, although no one else did. She said that it was "like letting something out" when he opened that door. Or, perhaps, someone.

Staring up at the opening to the attic, I had the sense of relative safety up there, and then learned that two psychics had had the same feeling. They believed that the prostitutes would go up there to get away from their "business," or perhaps hide when there was trouble.

Once again, emotions and sensations were inundating us on many levels, and we decided to leave the brothel, for now, and return later to set up our cameras and meters. When we descended back into the bar, I was again concerned by how Mike appeared.

"You look very disturbed. You don't look like yourself," I said to him, with emphasis on not being himself. I was afraid one or more of the unearthly inhabitants were taking up residence in his head, and he finally admitted he was feeling very strange. Still, we continued, which in retrospect was probably not the wisest course of action under these bizarre circumstances. And it wasn't about to get any better.

Back in the bar area where we had left our equipment, I began getting things ready. A minute or two later I heard Mike calling my name, and found that he had gone down into the secret room to set up a camcorder. Sal showed me how to navigate the cramped closet and safely get my feet onto the narrow stairs. I thought Mike must have found something interesting he wanted to show me. Instead, I found him in a bad state.

He told me he felt very upset, agitated, almost panicky, and suddenly had a pounding headache. The small dark room did feel very unpleasant—and even as I write this I realize what a gross understatement that is—and I saw it was really affecting Mike in a negative way.

The stairs in the secret room. (Infrared image.)

"You should leave. This place is terrible and it's really getting to you," I told him.

"I know. That's why I called you down here so you could feel it, too," Mike said.

Despite the awful feeling in that room, I believe I smiled as I replied, "Thanks, I appreciate that."

Of course I understood his intentions; it just sounded kind of odd—"Hey, I feel really terrible, come on down so you can feel terrible, too!"

We got the camcorder up and running very quickly, then we headed for the stairs. As Mike was feeling the worst, I let him go first. However, once "out of the hole," he paused to talk with Sal, leaving me no room to get out. As I stood on the stairs, half in and half out, a wave of panic swept over me and I could have sworn someone was grasping my legs, trying to pull me back into the room

I tried to ignore the feeling, tried brushing the "hands" off my legs, but the feeling not only persisted, it intensified. I said, "I have the feeling someone is grabbing my legs," but Mike wasn't listening as he was speaking with Sal. I was about two seconds away from screaming at him to get out of the way (a phrase that would have included a choice obscenity) and shoving him as hard as I could, when he finally moved and I was able to pull my legs free. Thankfully, whatever had been grabbing at them stopped as soon as my legs were clear of that horrible secret room.

The incident really shook me up, and for several minutes I had a skin-crawling sensation on my legs. I found myself repeatedly trying to brush something away, although I knew that physically there wasn't anything there. I also came away with the distinct impression that more than just clandestine meetings took place in that room.

I would bet anything that people were roughed up down there, perhaps even severely beaten or killed, during the bootlegging days. It makes sense that the victims would have tried to escape up those stairs, and they would have been pulled back down by the "enforcers." Rationally, this is all speculation, but that terrifying feeling of someone trying to pull me down is all the convincing I require to believe that there is some truth to the theory.

I explained to Mike what I had just experienced, and how close he came to being shoved out of the way. In all of our years of working together under very stressful circumstances, we have never become angry or yelled at one another (unlike some of those awful "reality" ghost shows on television). Yet there I had been feeling panicked and on the verge of screaming at him. At that point I came to the realization that I was not myself, either. This time we agreed we both needed a break and went outside for some fresh air. Once outside, it was like crossing back into the normal world—such as it is—and it only reinforced the idea that paranormal activity runs rampant within the walls of Shanley's Hotel.

Our break over, and our heads partially cleared, we went back to work, and to minimize any sounds, Barbara, Sal and Cindy went into the apartment on the second floor. We quickly set up our equipment in the brothel, then Mike and I returned to the third floor with some meters and handheld cameras. After what we had experienced in the walkthrough, we were expecting to capture some impressive evidence.

So wouldn't you know, now that we had all of our equipment and were prepared for the actual investigation, *nothing* happened. We sat quietly in the various rooms that had evoked such strong reactions, and felt nothing, heard nothing, and saw nothing. It was hard to believe we were in the same place. I commented that it felt "like they had all gone into the woodwork." The same entities that had been bombarding us a short time ago appeared to be AWOL now that we were prepared to gather evidence of their existence.

Mike was drawn to one of the rooms in the front of the building, where he experienced bad feelings, but no more sounds. Again, it was as if all activity ceased as soon as we came to take a look. Mike finally said, "Give us a sign if you want us to leave. Bang something."

BANG!

Just a second after he said the words, there was a loud banging sound from somewhere close to us in the darkness.

"That was a bang! And it was not the plastic (on the windows)," I stated with confidence.

We were clearly not wanted any longer. But that didn't mean we were about to leave. Not by a long shot.

As we started descending the staircase to the second floor, Mike had the strong sensation that someone was standing right behind him. I took a few quick photos but nothing appeared, and as usual the feeling quickly passed. The paranormal cat and mouse game continued.

There were a few odd things on the second floor, but the moment that really got our attention came as we stood silently in the dark and a clock chimed loudly right next to us. We both jumped in surprise, and then laughed at having such a reaction to something solid and normal, with so much crazy paranormal activity all around us.

We decided to go back to the brothel and check out the rooms more thoroughly. I collected the meters and motion detectors we had set up earlier so we could move around without all kinds of alarms going off. We were both curious as to what was up in the attic, so Mike decided to use an old trick from previous investigations. He extended the legs of the tripod that held the camcorder, then raised it up like a periscope through the opening in the ceiling. I was standing behind him, watching, and we were both joking about the low-tech technique. At that point I was definitely not in a tense or anxious state by any means.

Then out of the blue there was this inexplicable sensation, like some bizarre shift in reality. In the blink of an eye I could have sworn the floorboards lifted up under my feet, sending me backwards into the wall. I felt woozy, disoriented, and nauseous. It was like falling into another world—a terrifying world I was afraid I couldn't return from. All I could say as I started reeling was, "Oh, boy…," and Mike turned in time to see me stumble backward and grab a chair to keep me from going down.

"What's the matter? What's the matter?" he asked with concern, not understanding what was happening, as he wasn't experiencing anything unusual. "Linda, are you all right?"

"Just lost it," I replied, not understanding what was happening to me, either, and having trouble finding words. "Just lost it, gotta get out of here."

My legs were shaky as I descended the steep staircase as quickly as I could, while keeping a tight grip on the railing with both trembling hands.

"Did it feel like something attacking you?" Mike asked.

"No, no…" I replied, still unable to describe the awful experience.

"Were there strong emotions?"

"No, it was just…everything shifted and I was just going off to another…Wow! I just couldn't stay on my feet…"

Mike urged me to sit down when we got back to the bar area, but I told him I was way too agitated.

"It was like the floor just moved," I tried to explain, not sure I was making any sense. "I mean, it didn't move, but it felt like…"

My words trailed off again as I paced back and forth, trying to clear my head. It had been as if reality itself had been pulled out from underneath me like a carpet, and I knew that in some sense I would never be the same. You just can't experience something that mind-blowing without having it leave a permanent impression.

It actually wasn't until a few days later when I was reviewing the audio recordings that I recalled having similar sensations the first time

I entered the brothel area, commenting several times about feeling like the floor was shifting and that I might fall. What bizarre forces are at work here? Does this lack of balance have anything to do with the objects that seem to suddenly balance in unnatural positions? Is this a result of the ghostly activity, or is the earth itself also exhibiting some strange natural forces here that we don't yet understand? And why did it have such an effect on me, yet Mike felt nothing just a couple of feet away? This phenomenon puzzles me more than anything I've yet encountered.

(Note: When I hit the floor at the suicide house [page 24] it was a completely different sensation. That involved an extremely emotional personal connection, and all of the experiences and reactions were internal. In this case at Shanley's, there were no corresponding thoughts or feelings, and the sensations appeared to be from external forces. In almost ten years of investigations I had never had these kind of experiences before, now there have been two cases just a few months apart where I had trouble staying on my feet—I sure hope this isn't going to become a trend!)

I needed to leave Shanley's ASAP, but there was still the camcorder down in the secret room. As much as Mike hated that room, he said he would retrieve the camera as I was still so shaken from my paranormal ordeal in the brothel, not to mention the awful feelings of being grabbed the last time I was in that horrible little room. However, a couple of minutes later, I heard him say, "I can't do it."

I walked around the corner and over to the closet, and found Mike standing there just staring at the dark opening in the floor.

"What's wrong?" I asked, anxious to get this over with.

"I just can't do it," he said with an odd expression, as if he was standing on the edge of a cliff and had been asked to jump.

I was still not myself, and was feeling exceptionally agitated and impatient, so I said I would do it. However, my attitude changed in a heartbeat as I stepped forward to the opening. As soon as I was directly above it, I was overwhelmed with sensations of dread and danger flowing out of the room, and I stopped short just as Mike had done. I looked back at him, hoping his spell had been broken, but he still was unable to move forward. I looked back into the foreboding darkness of the hole, and likened it to feeling as though I was about to plunge into a shark tank—and the sharks were very hungry…

Every shred of intuition and my self-preservation instincts told me to stay out of there. However, you don't do what I have done all these years without being very stubborn, and somewhat reckless.

*Suck it up, Zimmermann, and just do it!* I said to myself.

Taking a deep breath, I plunged into the opening and hurried down the narrow, steep stairs as quickly as possible. By the time my feet hit the debris-strewn floor in the dark, musty room, every sense was being assaulted. The spiritual sharks were in a feeding frenzy, but I was not going to run—at least not until I retrieved the camcorder. The adrenaline was pumping as I grabbed the camcorder and started back up the stairs. With each step up the sensations grew, as if whatever forces at work were increasing their power to try to keep me down there.

Thrusting the camera out of the opening, Mike took hold of it so I had both hands free to hoist myself out of that evil black hole. As soon as I was completely clear, I hurried out of the closet to get away from those terrible feelings. Fortunately, nothing followed me out. But the psychic and psychological damage had been done. This was the last straw in a night of extraordinarily intense and stressful experiences. I was wasted and I was fried—stick a fork in me, because I was done!

Mike was equally fried, and I can't emphasize enough that I had never seen him so affected before. As we began packing up our equipment, he said something to the effect that if all the spirits wanted us to leave, they should have given us a sign. In an instant I "heard" a female voice in my head and started to repeat her words out loud.

"What the-" I stopped myself in considerable surprise and some embarrassment at what I was about to say to Mike in a rather nasty tone.

He looked at me with a puzzled expression, and once I regained my composure I explained that in response to his comment about giving us a sign to leave I was about to say, "What the **** do you think we've been doing!!!"

I also explained that although I was really stressed out, those words and that thought did not originate with me. They were really in my head now, and I was not happy. Barbara had told me that one of the female spirits was very "brassy" and had quite a vocabulary, and I don't doubt it! While I don't mind getting impressions at haunted locations, I most heartily object to being used in this manner.

We started packing even more quickly, and Barbara, Sal, and Cindy rejoined us. They were clearly surprised that we were leaving already, but we explained that we had more than enough for one night. However, despite all the trials and tribulations, we assured them that we would be back. If nothing else, curiosity would bring us back, not to mention our wounded pride at having been so vulnerable. Things would be different next time—at least we hoped so!

As we left, I asked Mike if he was okay to drive, as he was clearly not in a normal state of mind. He said he was okay, but as he spoke I knew he was still very much "under the influence" of everything that had just happened. We were both still reeling from the ordeal, and during the drive back we tried to take a rational look at what had transpired, with little success. About the only thing we could conclude with any certainty was that we were probably both in for a wild night's sleep.

When I got home the first thing I did was throw my dusty and dirty clothes in the washing machine, then I took a long, hot shower. I was so wound up that sleep did not come easily, and when it finally came it was not pleasant. Several times I actually woke up screaming from nightmares of people chasing at attacking me at Shanley's. The same dreams repeated themselves throughout the night. When morning finally arrived I wondered if anyone had gotten the license plate number of the paranormal truck that had run over me.

Mike and I went back to Shanley's in May, and again in June, to give lectures, and lead some ghost hunts. We experienced the same unpleasant feelings in the same places, but at least I didn't fall down again!

What I found most interesting was a group I took up to the brothel, which was composed predominantly of women. I hadn't told them anything about my feelings of disorientation and troubles standing up straight, as I wanted to hear unbiased reactions. Almost immediately the women in the group felt uncomfortable, and somewhat disoriented. Then one woman complained that the floor seemed to be moving.

"It's like trying to stand on the deck of a ship," she said with her arms out as if trying to steady herself.

Bingo! So it wasn't my imagination. Even though others before me had experienced the unsteady sensation, it's always nice to get additional confirmation. It was also remarkable to find that while all of the women experienced some degree of these unusual feelings, the two men felt none of it. This is not to say that they were insensitive, because they experienced things in other parts of the house, but clearly women are most susceptible to whatever activity is at work in the former brothel.

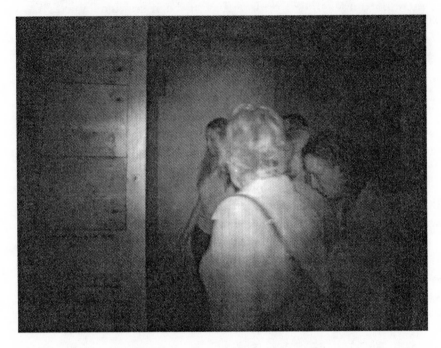

The women in the brothel who also felt as if the floor was moving.
(Infrared image.)

Another dramatic event occurred in the secret room. Mike had brought several people down there and one woman felt something touching her. Then half her body got hot, while the other felt icy cold. (There isn't any source of heating or cooling in that room.) Using his non-contact thermometer, Mike was able to determine that her skin temperature was fifteen degrees different on the two sides of her body!

The hotel now hosts regular ghost hunts, so the body of paranormal evidence continues to grow. Psychic Lisa Ann shot an episode of *SCARED! TV* in the hotel in the summer of 2007, which will air in 2008. I don't want to scoop the show, but suffice to say she also encountered a variety of interesting ghosts throughout the place.

I am certain that this is not the end of the Shanley Hotel story, not by a long shot. Barbara has done an enormous amount of research on the history of the hotel, and it will be an ongoing project to try to unravel the mysteries of the many spirits who refuse to check out.

If you want to check in—and stay the night—the hotel should be opening as a bed and breakfast by the fall of 2007. If you aren't brave enough to spend an entire night, come by for a ghost hunt, or one of the special events or lectures. The Shanley Hotel represents a rare opportunity to experience firsthand an amazing paranormal world.

As their motto says, at the Shanley "The Spirits are Inn"!

For more information, go to www.shanleyhotel.com

The participants in our ghost hunt (not in order): Karen Moss, Elizabeth Benson, Jennifer Nolan, Evonne Benson, Claudia Zadro, Glen Macken, Judy Hazen, JoAnne Everett, Sarah Reyes, Mark VanEtter (and me kneeling in front).

# All Aboard!
## Ellenville, NY

Railroad Station, Ellenville, N. Y.

The Ellenville train station in the early 1900s.

There is nothing like getting more than you bargained for on a ghost hunt, even if it comes at the price of being terrified. I expected a fairly routine investigation of a fairly benign location, and what I got was one of my most remarkable experiences in over ten years of ghost hunting.

Barbara Bleitzhofer from Shanley's Hotel in Napanoch (see page 30) had told me that the old train station in Ellenville, New York, had some spirits of former employees lingering about the property. The station, built in 1905, is now a jewelry factory owned by Barbara Hoff, and Mike and I arranged to come by one Thursday evening in July of 2007.

The train station is deceptive in its appearance, and we were surprised by the many large rooms on several floors, as it has been modified and expanded over the decades. Barbara H. gave us a quick tour so we could orient ourselves, but I think we were even more disoriented at the end! However, that was nothing compared to what awaited us in the next building.

The structure had most recently been used for offices and a factory, but is now vacant. The instant I stepped inside, my guard went up and I commented that I didn't like this place at all. It was a bad feeling, plain and simple, and the unpleasant sensation persisted throughout our brief tour of the maze of empty rooms. Mike and I were not looking forward to investigating this building after dark.

There was yet another building to explore; the former freight station which is now a spacious antique store, with an expansive section the size of an airplane hangar. It has an entryway to the other building, which we didn't realize at the time, and during our walkthrough, everything seemed relatively peaceful and inactive—which would change later that evening.

The train station today, with it's many additions and changes.

Once we had a general idea what was where, Mike and I decided to start in the train station. Since there was so much area to cover, we also decided to go completely mobile this time, rather than set up equipment and leave it in various locations. We could always come back at another time and concentrate on any sections that seemed particularly active. The two Barbaras, and their friend, Betty Walsh, made themselves comfortable on some benches outside of the station, so whatever Mike and I might see or hear while inside could not be misconstrued. If something went "bump" that night, we could be certain it would be from the realm of the paranormal.

If something went "bang," or we heard footsteps and heavy objects being dragged, that would be considered paranormal as well, which is exactly what happened in one of the upstairs storerooms. As we opened one of the doors, Mike actually took a step back, as he had the overwhelming feeling that someone would be standing in the doorway. The room was empty, but there was a persistent sensation that we were not alone.

My general approach is to ask, "If anyone wants to make his presence known, give us a sign." However, this time I decided to ask, "Bang something to let us know you are here."

About two seconds later there was a loud sound, and I quickly acknowledged, "That was a bang!"

It was difficult to pinpoint where the sound had originated. I thought it was from the floor we were on, while Mike felt that it was somewhere downstairs. In any event, we didn't have time to ponder the location, because several seconds later the banging sound was followed by footsteps and the sound of something very heavy being dragged across the floor. We were above the old baggage area, so was this an echo from the past of someone's trunk or weighty luggage being carried? We tried to follow the sounds, but they stopped and we just couldn't place them.

The former ticket office is also a room of interest. We found a circular area of high EMF readings in the center of the floor, and it is apparently a section the employees refer to as a "dead spot," because sounds seem to be unnaturally muffled here. The woman who works at the far end of the room is always startled when someone comes to her workbench, because she never hears anyone approaching through that dead spot. Perhaps the name means more than they imagine?

The former ticket window. (Infrared image.)

When Mike and I were in the room, the clock by the workbench started making a fairly loud grinding sound. I commented that I couldn't imagine anyone being able to concentrate with that annoying noise, and it was no wonder that the woman who sat here never heard anyone approach. Mike countered by telling me that he had made a phone call in this room just before our investigation started and he was absolutely certain the clock was not making that noise. I asked where he was standing at the time, and it was not more than four feet from the clock.

Later, we asked Barbara H. about the clock, and she said it would occasionally make an odd sound for a second or two, but never anything that loud, and definitely never such a prolonged grinding noise, which ended up lasting for hours (it was still making the sound when we left). Perhaps whatever spirit resides here was trying to impress upon us the importance of time and keeping to schedules? Punctuality was a virtue in the world of the railroad, and what better way to let us know that a man who lived and breathed timetables was still present? Barbara B. has seen and felt a rather fussy man in a railroad uniform in this area, a man who doesn't like people interfering with his "work," so it's also possible he was signaling for us to not waste his valuable time!

In another storage area, we were surprised when a door slammed right behind us as I was opening another door. It was startling, but when we recreated the situation, it appeared as though air pressure had been the cause of the door seeming to close on its own. Disappointing, but you always have to search for a rational explanation before jumping to any paranormal conclusions. And speaking of jumping…

There were a few other odd noises and strange sensations throughout the building, but the real thrill was to be found in the former train station waiting room. The place where countless people awaited the arrival of loved ones and passengers strained to hear the whistle of their approaching train is now a jewelry showroom containing hundreds of pairs of earrings and bracelets on racks and display stands.

When Mike and I entered the room, we admired the architecture and the original paint. Then, as I was in the process of saying, "Can anyone make something move?" I stopped abruptly before saying the word "move." The reason I stopped was because out of the corner of my eye I saw some movement, and when I turned there was a heavy chain bracelet swinging back and forth on a display!

The arrow points to the heavy chain bracelet that was vigorously
swinging back and forth. (Infrared image.)

Mike's camcorder was not on, but we quickly snapped some
digital still photos in infrared. Not quite the same thing as capturing
the actual motion, but we did want to see if anything else might be
captured. As soon as the bracelet stopped moving, I attempted to
recreate the movement to see if it was caused by anything we had done.

I blew directly at the hanging bracelet to see if a breeze possibly created by our entering had caused the motion, but I had to blow very hard at less than a foot away to get it to budge. We had been at least ten feet away when we first saw it moving.

Next, we checked for loose floorboards to see if vibration from our footsteps had been the cause. Walking back and forth, we found that the old station floor was remarkably well built. It was solid and sturdy, and even when I began jumping up and down, not a single piece of jewelry moved. It was not the most dignified looking action, but it clearly proved the point.

Speaking of single pieces, it's important to note that had some natural air current or vibration been sufficient to set that heavy bracelet swinging vigorously back and forth, there were hundreds of other much lighter pieces of jewelry that should have also been set in motion. Yet there it was, just that one bracelet swinging, and just as I was about to ask for some type of movement as an indication that a spirit was present.

"That was impressive!" I concluded with satisfaction. An object moving is a rare event, so I was quite pleased to have witnessed such a phenomenon.

Hoping that we could witness the event again, I sat down on the floor about ten feet from the bracelet display, while Mike stood nearby with a camcorder ready. The bracelet didn't move, but as if on cue when I asked for something else to move, I saw that a single jeweled earring was now swinging back and forth, reflecting the dim evening light like a paranormal beacon. Again, this earring was on a rack with dozens of earrings, but somehow, only this one was in motion.

"Behind you, Mike, behind you!" I said with excitement. "An earring is moving!"

"Where?" he asked, as I realized that saying "an earring behind you" was akin to saying "a piece of hay in that stack." There were many racks stretching the length of the long counter, each one filled with rows of earrings.

I refined my description to the specific rack, and how many rows down I thought it was located. Mike aimed his camcorder in the general direction, but the bright infrared light reflected off of hundreds of beads, crystals, and bits of shiny metal in the racks of earrings, so it was impossible to pick out the one I saw moving.

A minute or so later, Mike asked, "Move something or give us a sign of your presence so we have no doubt."

About three seconds later there was a metallic clinking sound about six feet behind us. I was suddenly covered in goose bumps, and we immediately turned, but didn't see anything moving as this area was in darkness. After the investigation we came back and tapped on several pieces of the jewelry in that section and actually found a large necklace that made the exact sound. But that sound could only have been created by someone physically pushing the piece of jewelry, or a strong gust of wind—of which neither scenario had occurred when we heard the clinking sound.

Two objects that we witnessed moving, and one that we heard, all on the same investigation! This was indeed impressive. However, as amazing as this was, we were about to be impressed in another way, and it wouldn't be good…

The next phase of the investigation was the building in which we were not comfortable, to say the least. Almost immediately we had EMF readings and I asked, "Does anything want to make its presence known…in a nice way?"

I felt I needed to add those last words because it seemed as though we were in the midst of something harmful. We moved slowly around the several front rooms where the feeling was the strongest, until Mike stopped and complained of head pain. Taking a deep breath, he turned his back against the wall as if in preparation of being confronted. We both began speaking to whatever was present in a demanding and aggressive tone, and I said to Mike, "We aren't even acting like ourselves."

He didn't reply and looked as though his thoughts were very far away, and the expression on his face became dark and menacing— something I had never seen before.

"Mike, are you all right?" I asked, but he made no reply. "You don't look good. You're scaring me."

I was serious, too. The look on his face was threatening, and for a moment I was concerned that he had fallen under a very bad influence. I actually started backing away from him, but fortunately he snapped out of it. He explained that he felt threatened and was "on guard." He compared it to the feeling of responding to a call of a break-in, and being prepared at any moment for an assailant to come out of the shadows.

After that disturbing episode we chose to move on, and just hoped that the negative influence was restricted to those few rooms.

Wishful thinking...

Out of the blue, Mike said that whatever this entity or entities were, they were not related to the building, that it was something attached to the property from an earlier time. I felt that over the years it must have influenced whoever stayed or worked here, making them do bad things they normally would not do. The negative presence had plainly already had an impact on us, and our normal benign approach to investigations became adversarial. It was us against "them", but we were determined to continue and try to get answers, no matter what happened.

In retrospect, it was not really the smartest move. It's probably best to walk away from such things, but instead we went deeper into the large building with its maze-like floor plan.

Next we came upon a room with a flickering fluorescent light. Neither of us had turned on any lights, and we later confirmed that on our initial walkthrough, no one had touched any switches because there was still bright sunshine outside. We found the switch on the opposite wall, which further confirmed that none of us had turned on the light, because during our walkthrough no one entered that room.

In the room next door we found a dead bird that something had been chewing on—nothing paranormal, but it certainly didn't help our state of mind.

My skin was really crawling at this point, and I reiterated what I had felt the first time I entered the building—there was a "cult-like" feel to the influences at work here. It may not have been the most eloquent way of putting it, but I stated that I felt as though "they ceremonially did bad things to people." I paused a moment and then added, "And they don't like you."

"No, they don't," Mike agreed, still feeling on edge and threatened.

A moment later, we both literally got that skin-crawling sensation that we often describe as feeling like cobwebs all over your skin. This was a section that we had all passed through before, so if there had been any real cobwebs we should have felt them then, and knocked them away.

The feeling persisted and grew in intensity. Using a bright Maglite flashlight, I carefully searched my arms and the ceiling for any sign of dust or webs, and found nothing. Mike was really affected, but I couldn't see a thing on him, either. The presence of the predominant entity grew stronger, and all I could say was that this feeling was "awful."

My scalp even began to tingle in a most unpleasant manner, and poor Mike felt this sensation everywhere and tried desperately to wipe away something that most likely didn't exist, in a physical form at least. Even standing still he felt whatever it was moving across his body. There was one moment of comic relief as we swatted at the air and rubbed our arms, faces, hands, and backs.

"We must look like idiots!" I said.

The laughter momentarily eased the tension, but finally, the crawling sensation became unbearable and we had to move away from that spot. And just to compare and contrast: later on Mike walked into an actual spider web, but it clearly felt like a web and we could clearly see the strands in the beam of the flashlight. This other feeling has no visible source.

Unfortunately, the feeling continued to follow Mike, and nothing we did could stop it. In addition, as he passed through a doorway something tapped him on the top of his head and the air seemed to turn colder. I placed my Trifield meter in the doorway, and Mike stood on one side, while I stood on the other, at least six feet away.

After zeroing out any naturally occurring EM fields, we just stood and waited for any reaction. We didn't have to wait long. The meter began to register some type of energy, and I decided on a little Q&A.

"Are you a man?"

There was a slight buzzing sound from the meter.

"That wasn't very strong, can you—"

I didn't get a chance to continue because the meter made a loud buzzing sound and I actually saw the needle move up the scale, which meant some substantial energy was present.

"Okay, that was strong!" I said, encouraged to continue.

"So you were a man," I repeated as the meter once again buzzed. "And you victimized people?"

I'm still not sure why I said those specific words, but the meter really buzzed frighteningly loudly, and the needle registered the highest reading so far. Given the nature of this Q&A, I wasn't quite sure that I was happy about getting such definitive responses!

I tried to pin down an approximate date for this entity at this location, but not until I asked, "Are you something that was here before this building was built" did I get a definitive reaction, and then what a reaction I got!

The meter squealed as the meter spiked high, dropped, and spiked again for at least ten seconds, unlike anything I had ever seen before. I gasped, and was covered with goose bumps. Whatever this was had energy that could pack a wallop!

From that point, the energy level continued to rise and fall over and over, and it became impossible to pose anymore questions. I asked for a sign other than the meter, and a few moments later I heard a sigh or whisper. I asked Mike if it was him, and he said no. When I played to audio back later, there is some kind of sound that can be heard over the squealing Trifield, but it's impossible to make out any details.

"Was that you making that sound?" I posed to the energetic spirit. Again the meter had a record-breaking reaction. We were truly witnessing something unique, bizarre, and unnerving. The meter finally grew silent, and we decided to move upstairs.

It took us a while to find the staircase, and when we started to ascend I mentioned that I felt as though someone was constantly following me. No sooner had I finished my sentence when there was some kind of banging or footsteps directly behind me.

Mike remarked, "You just said that and then there was the sound!"

And no sooner had he finished his sentence when the same sound occurred again. This time we stopped in our tracks and waited, but nothing else happened there. We continued on to a huge, empty storage area that had another staircase leading up to a large attic. There were some really bad feelings around that staircase.

"Do we want to go up there?" I asked.

Mike took a deep breath before replying, "I don't know. How do you feel? I don't know if I want to do it."

"All right," I said, not at all upset that we didn't have to go up there.

"Do you feel like going?" Mike asked.

"I am *not* thrilled about the idea," I emphasized, but left the possibility open.

Taking another deep breath, Mike said in a resigned manner, "Well, we are here, and this is what we are here for."

"Yeah, I know," I said in probably the least enthusiastic tone I could manage.

It's kind of like getting an injection, or something else you know is going to be unpleasant, but you have to do it. This *was* what we were here for, but we certainly didn't have to like it.

Slowly and carefully we made our way up the stairs. Actually, once we got to the top it didn't feel so bad. We agreed it felt much better than anywhere else to this point, and speculated that whatever nasty presence or presences are in the building, they don't come up to the top level. But that was where the good news ended, because we both heard several loud noises from the bottom of the staircase we had just come up.

"Oh crap!" I said in disgust, and mild fear, "We have to go back down those stairs."

Mike just groaned. Neither of us wanted to face whatever was waiting for us, but it was our only way down. However, before taking a single step, I suggested we put away our meters and cameras and leave both hands free to tightly grip the railing as we descended. Mike did not disagree. In fact, he had just been about to suggest the same thing.

I volunteered to go first, and I took one careful step at a time, all the while with something of a death grip on the railing. We were both getting the feeling that someone wanted nothing more than to have us fall, and would resort to pushing us if possible.

I had to resist the strong impulse to rush down as fast as I could, because I knew that could be disastrous. Still, it was torture moving this slowly when every self-preservation instinct said *run!*

I had a small flashlight clipped to my vest (I wear a SWAT vest with plenty of pockets for instruments and cameras) that lighted my way, and Mike had his bright flashlight as he began his descent. When I was just a few steps from the bottom, I glanced over toward the doorway about thirty feet away and saw a dark shadowy figure. It was just a few feet inside of the door near the wall, and when I took a good look it seemed to rush out the door. Even though it was very brief, it was very clear. At first I thought it was my own shadow being generated from Mike's flashlight, so I didn't get very excited.

However, when I looked back and saw that Mike wasn't even halfway down the staircase, I began to question that theory. Once we were both down and had a moment to take a few breaths, we tried a little experiment. Mike went back up to where he was on the staircase when I saw the shadow and I resumed my place a few stairs up. First of all, the way Mike had been holding his light, my shadow would have been directly in front of me, not thirty feet to my right.

He tried shining his flashlight at all different angles, and we were finally able to get my shadow to appear by the doorway, but it was a huge gray image at least ten feet high and wide, and quite ill-defined. What I saw was a normal human height and width, very dark, with well-defined outlines. There was simply no way to reproduce the image I saw with Mike's flashlight, given the distance and our positions.

When I realized that, my blood ran cold at what I had witnessed. Had our "companion" materialized in hopes of seeing one of us fall? Or was it given the strength to appear by feeding off of our fear? They were chilling thoughts, and we had just one too many chilling thoughts during this phase of the investigation.

We needed out!

Unfortunately, that would not be easy.

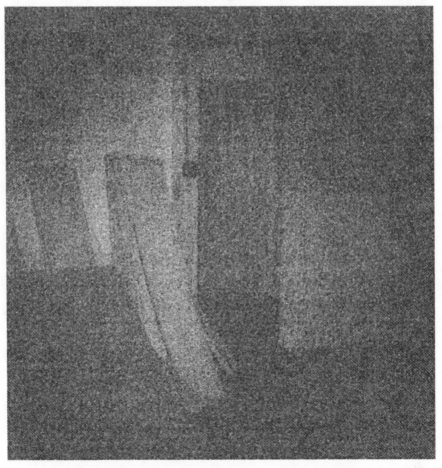

The doorway where I saw the figure. (Infrared image.)

We made our way back down to the ground floor and looked

forward to that wonderful moment when we exited this awful, awful building. I reached out to the doorknob and almost collided with the door because it didn't budge, and Mike almost collided with me as we came to a sudden dead stop.

Stepping back, I took a quick look behind me to make sure this was the way we had come in. It was the door through which we had entered, so I tried turning the knob and pushing harder. No movement whatsoever.

"We're locked in," I said, slightly perturbed, but not yet afraid, as I thought that for some reason the owner had come over and locked the door behind us.

"Why would she do that?" Mike asked, equally unhappy with the prospect of spending another minute in that place.

The unpleasant presence felt particularly strong at that moment, and we were getting antsy, to say the least, but still I assumed all we had to do was turn the deadbolt to get out. I grabbed a hold of it and tried twisting it one way, then the other. It didn't budge.

"Mike, we *are* locked in here, and I don't think the owner did it," I said, genuinely feeling some pangs of fear. I felt trapped, as if whatever had been tormenting us wanted very much to keep us inside to continue his game.

Mike stepped forward and also tried turning the deadbolt, with no success.

"We *are* locked in! Oh my god, we can't get out! Quick, take a picture!"

Despite our predicament, he had the presence of mind to suggest taking pictures to document the moment, and possibly catch our tormenter in the act. But we didn't have any time to review the photographs. We *had* to get out of there!

I could see the three women were still sitting several hundred feet away by the train station. I hoped they would be able to hear me as I started knocking on the glass. Thankfully, they looked over, but then to our dismay they all just smiled and waved.

"They don't get it!" I said, my voice rising in fear, as I tried tugging on the door with all of my strength.

I will never forget that image—Mike and I are seconds away from a full-fledged panic, I'm banging on the door as if to save my life, and there was Barbara B. grinning, her arm reaching high, waving as if nothing in the world was wrong. We were going down for the count, and they were all smiles, blissfully unaware that we had been locked in by a deranged spirit. We laughed about it later, but at that moment it wasn't the least bit funny.

I started pounding even more frantically, and I didn't realize that behind me Mike was using his flashlight to try to signal S.O.S., or at least something similar! Finally, Barbara B. realized that we must be locked in (or completely out of our minds), and Barbara H. got up and started to walk over. If she had run as fast as she could it wouldn't have been fast enough.

Climbing the steps to the door, she reached up with her key, but then stopped. I couldn't understand what she was doing, but then she simply grabbed the doorknob, pushed gently, and the door easily swung open! The door which had been locked so tightly that two desperate adults couldn't get it open, was suddenly unlocked without the need of a key, and opening with no effort! How could that be?

"Did you lock us in here?" I asked as Mike and I hurried outside.

"No, we've all been sitting over there the entire time," she replied, clearly not quite understanding what all the fuss was about.

We explained to everyone that neither of us had touched the lock when we entered, and that the door had somehow locked itself and we couldn't unlock it no matter how hard we tried. I didn't want to be rude about the situation, but I had to ask them all to swear that no one locked that door behind us, and they all swore that they hadn't even left their seats.

So there it was—Mike and I had been locked into a building by a threatening presence that appears as a dark form! Words really can't describe how we felt, but "totally freaked out" would be a start. When I got home, I was able to confirm in my photo that the deadbolt was in the

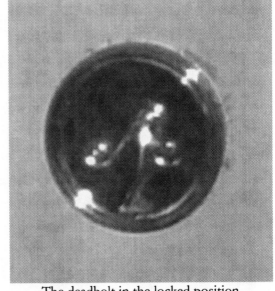
The deadbolt in the locked position.

locked position. This was without a doubt one of the most amazing things to ever happen to us on an investigation, not to mention one of the most frightening.

"I am *not* going back in there tonight," Mike said, then added, "I am *never* going back in there."

We were both really shaken by what had just transpired, and I didn't hesitate to agree with him. However, there was still one building left, the old freight building, and it had an inside entrance to the "bad" building, but maybe it would be completely different?

After a break to catch our breath and renew our courage, we cautiously entered the enormous freight building. Unfortunately, as soon as we walked in we both felt that same awful presence, not to the same intensity level, but uncomfortably there nonetheless. And as the lights were on, one of us had to go into the back corner to the switches. Those switches happened to be located next to the wood and glass doors at the inside entrance to the other building.

I looked at Mike, he looked at me, and neither of us was moving any closer to that back corner. He clearly did not want to even be in this building, so as uneasy as I felt, I went for the lights.

How did it feel approaching those doors and looking back into the building from which we had just escaped? Something of a cross between the dentist coming at you with his drill, and entering a funhouse wondering what would be jumping out at you. I was actually surprised, and quite relieved, that I didn't see that dark figure peering at me through the glass. Still, I felt awful just being so close again, and quickly hurried back to where Mike was standing.

"You know, I think it's in here right now with us," Mike said, echoing my feelings.

"I know. Let's just do a quick walkthrough then," I said. "Of course, we don't even have to stay in here. What do you think?"

"Maybe just a walkthrough," Mike replied with some hesitation. "I don't know if I'm up to opening my mind to this again."

Even though we had agreed to do a walkthrough, neither of us actually started walking.

"How about we just stand by the door and ask some questions?" I suggested. "That's about all I'm up for. How about you?"

Mike agreed with no hesitation this time.

"We'll stand right here," I said moving back toward the door. "And if this door ends up getting locked, I quit ghost hunting!"

We both took deep breaths, and I began again.

"Okay, I hate to ask, but does anything want to make its presence known?" I said only half-joking.

"Did you follow us in here?" Mike asked.

There were no outward signs, but Mike's skin started to crawl again, and I was definitely back on high alert. We tried a few more questions, but didn't receive any clear responses, other than becoming increasingly uncomfortable. We decided we would move from the door, and go into the section that looked like an airplane hangar. It was actually yet another attached building, and we hoped that, as it was even farther away, the bad influence might be diminished there, or even better, gone.

When we entered, we found that a large light was on, high up on the ceiling. I had wanted to take some pictures in infrared, but we couldn't find the switch to turn it off. We both stood under the light for a few minutes, until we heard movement in the far corner, about fifty feet away. Rats, perhaps?

A few moments later there were more sounds, but these were definitely like the footsteps of an adult, accompanied by what sounded like heavy objects being pushed or pulled across the floor. There had to be an intruder lurking in the shadows!

Running over, we scanned the few boxes and objects leaning against the walls, and found no one. There simply wasn't anywhere to hide, and we couldn't understand what was happening. The sounds were so loud and clear, maybe someone was walking along the outside of the metal wall, and the sounds were carrying?

It seemed like a plausible theory, until we heard the footsteps moving behind us, definitely *inside* the building. Turning quickly, we still didn't see anyone or anything moving in the mostly empty old building. But someone *was* in there with us, and it felt uncomfortably like the presence from the other building. It also sounded like it moved back into the antiques section, where we had to go in order to get out.

"Great, here we go again," I said, dreading having to pass through another gauntlet of paranormal sensations.

"Don't worry. I'll go first...right after you!" Mike joked.

We walked through the wide doorway together, secured the heavy

71

door, then paused to see if anything would happen. All seemed quiet, until Mike asked if whatever was there wanted us to leave.

A chill shot through me and I got the distinct impression of an "evil grinning face" and the words, "No, I want you to *come back*!"

Maybe I was under too much strain and imagining the whole thing, but in any event, that was the last straw.

"Don't say that!" Mike said after I told him. "I have chills all over my body."

"Me, too. That's it, I'm getting out of here. Stick a fork in us, we're done!" I said as we reached the door. Mercifully, it opened and we quickly moved outside. We both breathed deep sighs of relief.

"I guess we survived to ghost hunt another day," Mike concluded.

The three women were still sitting on the benches, and we filled them in on what had transpired. I asked if they had seen anyone walking along the back corner of the building where we heard the noises, but they assured us no one else had been nearby.

We thought the night was finally over, when Barbara H. said, "Did you guys leave some equipment in there?"

She was pointing to the airplane hangar section, where light was clearly visible in the high windows.

"No, that's not our light," I replied. "That's the light up on the ceiling."

She looked at me with an odd, puzzled expression.

"In the two years we have been in that building, we have never had that light on. We didn't even know there was a light! We've been looking, but never found a switch," she explained to our surprise.

The news was both unexpected and disturbing—this meant that we would have to go back in there to try to turn it off. The only switches I had touched were the ones to turn off the lights in the antiques section, but perhaps one of those switches turned on the light in the hangar building?

"Ohhhh, nooooo, we have to go back in," I said, thinking of the image of the grinning face that wanted us to return.

"You were right!" Mike said. "Something does want us in there."

Fortunately, Barbara H. accompanied us back inside, and we left the door propped open this time. Mike and I stayed kind of close to the open door, and Barbara H. went to the switches. She tried them one by one, and we called out to Barbara B. to let us know when the hangar light was off. Oddly, it didn't appear that any of the switches controlled that particular light, but a few moments after, Barbara B. shouted over to us that the light was now out. We didn't care how it had gone out, just as long as it had.

Relieved once again, we left the building and headed toward the benches. We hadn't gone more than a few feet when Barbara B. saw that the light in the hangar section came back on! It wanted us back inside again!

"No way, I'm not going back in there," Mike stated firmly.

"I'm not going in there either," I said.

At this point, everyone's nerves were rattled, and even Barbara H. said that she didn't want to go back in, and would just leave the light on until morning, if she could finally locate the switch then.

"You can burn out the light bulb," I said toward the building. "We are *not* coming back in."

With that, we turned our backs and called it a night.

And what a night! What a study in contrasts, and what a variety of activity! Ghost hunting doesn't get much better than this, or worse, depending on how you look at it. We witnessed objects moving, saw a dark figure, heard numerous sounds, got inexplicable EMF readings that seemed to come in response to our questions, felt threatened, got locked in, and had a light go on by itself, at least twice.

Mike and I were stressed out to a remarkable degree from our ordeal, but it was all worth it for this amazing evidence. From hoping that we might capture some slight signs of the spirits of former railroad employees still on the premises, to having our emotional and psychic doors blown off (or locked down, as the case may be), was just more than we could process that night.

Still, weeks later, as I listen to the audio recordings, watch the tapes again, and write this story, the feelings and sensations all come rushing back with great clarity and impact. It was one wild night, and I will not soon forget what we went through.

Do the spirits of former railroad workers linger here? Is there also something darker, something from a time before the railroad? I would have to say yes to both questions.

Will I do another investigation at this location? Well, given what transpired, I don't think I'll be getting tickets for a return trip anytime soon…

# Shadowland
## Ellenville, New York

If ever there was an appropriate name for a haunted location, it is the Shadowland Theater on Canal Street in Ellenville, New York. The theater opened its art deco-style doors on July 3, 1920, and offered a mixture of silent films and live entertainment. A devastating fire gutted the structure in November of 1937, but it was rebuilt and continues to operate to this day.

The Shadowland Theater in the early days of its operation.
Courtesy of the Ellenville Public Library & Museum

Special thanks to Harley Bleitzhofer for obtaining the photos from the library.

In a building dedicated to the art of illusion and fictional realities, Shadowland presents something above and beyond standard theater fair—there are shadows of the dead here who still appear to the living and make themselves known in quite a variety of ways.

Objects are constantly being moved, and not in a manner that can be explained by absentmindedness, or by a coworker simply borrowing something and leaving it in another location. Two prime examples: During construction, a set builder left his hammer on the stage when everyone quit for the evening. In the morning it was not where he had left it, and after a thorough search it was simply nowhere to be found—until someone looked up. There about forty feet high on the ceiling was the hammer, dangling from the lighting framework! Needless to say, no one had brought in a cherry picker in the middle of the night so it was not humanly possible for someone to have put the hammer up there.

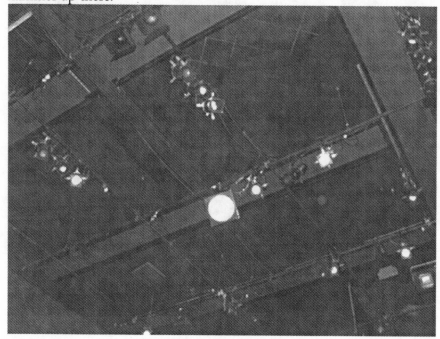

How could a hammer end up dangling from this high ceiling?

Another impossible feat occurred just a few months ago before a performance that required a gun. They used a real revolver loaded with blanks which was kept securely locked in a safe. Only two people had a key: the prop manager and the actor who would pull the trigger. The prop manager had carefully put all the bullets in the chamber of the gun and then locked it in the safe. Right before the scene during the play that required the shooting, the actor used his key to open the safe. The gun was in there, but all the blanks had been removed and placed next to the gun!

Was this just a paranormal prank, or was there some deeper message to removing bullets from a gun?

The seats and balcony as they once looked.
Courtesy of the Ellenville Public Library & Museum

Theaters are all about drama, and what could be more dramatic than choosing to end your life by committing suicide in a carefully staged manner? A woman did just that several decades ago. She had come to the theater to watch a performance, and then apparently hid somewhere inside while everyone filed out at the end of the show. The next day, horrified employees found the woman hanging from the ceiling above the balcony. No one ever discovered why she did it, or why she chose Shadowland as the place to end it all.

Or did it all end?

Over the years, actors onstage have reported seeing a woman hanging above the balcony. People have also heard whispering when no one is up there. The balcony no longer has seats, but is used to store racks of costumes. I found that when I was there, the dense walls of fabric muffled sound quite effectively, so normal whispering in the balcony should not carry throughout the theater.

The night of the investigation, Bob and I were accompanied by Barbara Bleitzhofer, her son Jacob, and his girlfriend Erica Green, who volunteers at the theater. Erica described an unusual event with one of the heavy racks of clothes, each of which must weigh a few hundred pounds, and are not easily moved (I gave one a shove and it barely wavered). In front of several witnesses, the end of one of the pipes that hold the clothes suddenly "jumped" upward about a foot. A tremendous burst of energy was required to either pull or push that pipe, and no one was within arm's reach at the time.

The heavy costume racks on the balcony.

Behind that rack are metal ducts, and several people have reported hearing children under the ducts. There is nothing on record about any children dying on the premises since the building has been a theater, but the building itself is much older, so who can tell what occurred there before?

Several things of interest occurred to us that night in the balcony. Using the digital EMF meter, Bob found an area of high readings, which also fluctuated significantly. The area would probably have corresponded to the spot below where the woman had hung herself, but we can't be sure. What we could be certain of was the meter, which continued to display readings that rose and fell for no apparent reason.

I went to the edge of the balcony to take a picture looking up at the suicide location, which today is covered by a drop ceiling. It was dark, but my camera sees in infrared. I aimed my camera upward, but didn't take a picture because there was a large circle of light on the ceiling. Thinking that someone was using their flashlight, I patiently waited for area of the light (which was over a two feet in diameter) as it moved slowly to my right, then back to my left, and then finally disappeared from the viewfinder. Then I took the picture.

When I lowered my camera, I saw that Bob was still monitoring the meter, and everyone else was at the back of the balcony near the door, where they would not have had a good angle with their flashlights to make the circular pattern of light I witnessed.

"Was anyone just shining their flashlight on the ceiling above me here?" I asked.

Everyone replied that they hadn't. I had a slight tinge of annoyance with myself, and again asked if everyone was certain that the beams of their flashlights could not have accidentally passed along the ceiling a few seconds earlier. Barbara, Jacob, and Erica's flashlights hadn't even been on, and Bob's flashlight was pointed down at the EMF meter the entire time. Now I was really annoyed.

There had been a large circle of light I was actually witnessing in infrared slowly moving for several seconds in an area where a woman had committed suicide, and I *waited for it to go away* before I took a picture! Ugh. This goes on my list of "Not So Great Moments in Ghost Hunting History." After all, who wants to capture a phantom light on camera?

I waited and waited for the light to reappear, but of course, it never did. There was one more inexplicable occurrence, however. While I was at the edge of the balcony, I clearly heard a woman's voice down below. It sounded like she was in a room, or perhaps outside speaking loudly. The only problem with that was that no one else was in the building, and voices from the outside apparently do not travel through the thick brick walls.

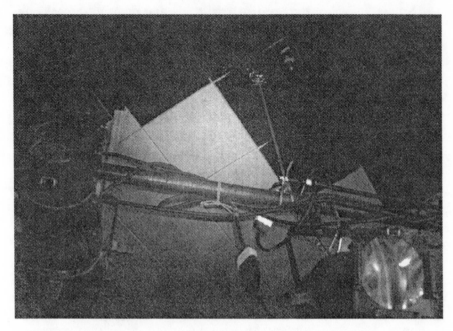

This balcony ceiling covers the area where the woman hung herself. This photo was taken just after I saw the large light moving.

Our next stop was the restroom area. Many people over the years have reported doors opening and closing in the two restrooms, and then finding that no one else was there. I didn't find anything unusual, but I did admire the original art deco signs. I appreciate unique fonts, and you can't beat the style of the lettering in the 1920s and 30s.

The original restroom sign.

Next, we went onto the stage and it was hard not to imagine what this place must have looked like in its heyday. What classic movies were shown here, what actors and actresses thrilled audiences? And of greatest importance, who still walks that stage in the dead of night, and what lost souls still sit in the seats and wander the aisles trying to recapture the enjoyment they once experienced here?

The stage, in its prime, and fallen into disrepair.
Courtesy of the Ellenville Public Library & Museum

An infrared image of the dressing rooms under the stage.

For starters, I would venture to say that at least one man still struts across this stage. The reason I say that is because I heard him.

There are dressing rooms under the stage that can be reached from an outside door, or from a narrow staircase under a set of pipes that isn't used anymore because you need to be something of a contortionist to get down them (I guess there's no need to say which way I decided to take).

As I reached the bottom of the staircase, there were five or six heavy footsteps above me, and it sounded like a man in hard soled shoes or boots.

"You're walking around up there?" I shouted back up the stairs, just to confirm that it was one of the living who made the distinct footsteps.

"No, we're all sitting on the couch," Barbara replied, referring to herself, Jacob, and Erica. Bob was on the stairs behind me, so it couldn't have been him, either.

'No! No way!' I replied in great surprise, and then went on to describe what I had just heard.

When I came back up onto the stage, I took a look at the shoes everyone was wearing, and it was sneakers all the way around, so they couldn't have possibly made the sounds of a man in boots. But obviously, something did!

We went down into the rows of seats, and Barbara said that on several occasions she had seen a figure come around the corner, down the aisle, and sit in the end seat of the third row from the back (seat E14 of the center section if you would like to try it). Bob placed the digital EMF meter there and again got high, fluctuating readings. I set the Trifield meter on the armrest and sat on the floor about eight feet away.

We asked a series of questions with no response, but when I asked if this spirit was from the early days of the theater the meter alarm squealed loudly. About the same time, Erica felt a jolt of energy and Barbara was pushed by something that couldn't be seen. There was also a sound of paper hitting the floor, something light, like a theater program perhaps?

There were several other bursts of energy registered by the meters, but then the activity ceased. Had there been some natural source of these readings, they would have continued.

We carried on with the investigation, checking out an assortment of small rooms and corridors. There was the occasional odd sound, fleeting reading, and passing thought or emotion. Nothing was overwhelming, but it was persistent. Barbara continued to sense and see a variety of spirits all around us, which was not surprising.

I next went down into the prop basement with Erica and Jacob. There was nothing unusual, except that a couple of lights were on that none of us had turned on, and despite tracing the lines, we couldn't find any switches to turn them off. Perhaps this wasn't paranormal in itself, but the fact that they were on when they should have been off was one more strange piece of the Shadowland puzzle.

Barbara at seat E14. (Infrared image.)

Finally, Bob and I went back to the balcony and spent some time in the quiet darkness. Well, it was quiet most of the time, except when we heard what sounded like someone moving around in the theater below us (everyone else was sitting in the lobby), and the loud banging sound in the ceiling above us. The EMF meters continued to pick up fluctuating EM fields, as well.

All things considered, it was a satisfying night of investigating.

Are there ghosts in the Shadowland Theater? I would have to say yes, there are most likely several spirits that are there for a variety of reasons. Fortunately, though understandably unnerving for some people, these are not malicious ghosts and at no time was there the slightest feeling of being threatened—which was a refreshing change of pace for me!

Theaters are the stuff of dreams; dreams both fulfilled and shattered. If ghosts search for something in death that they could not find in life, what better place than this to find answers in the tragedies and comedies displaying the wide range of human nature.

If you attend a performance at the Shadowland Theater, just keep in mind that what you might first think is a unique lighting technique or an unusual looking actor may just actually be a glimpse of the paranormal. And if you chose center aisle seat E14, remember you may not be sitting alone…

The former concession area.
Courtesy of the Ellenville Public Library & Museum

The main staircase, then and now.
Courtesy of the Ellenville Public Library & Museum

# Living with Death
## Middletown, NY

An early aerial view of the cemetery and surrounding land.

It's frightening enough to have someone banging violently on the front door of your house in the middle of the night, but when that house is in a cemetery, it's absolutely terrifying!

Chip Lewis had recently become caretaker of Walkill Cemetery in Middletown, New York, and he was sitting peacefully on his couch feeding his baby daughter. It was late, he didn't hear any cars pull up or any footsteps on the porch, yet suddenly someone was pounding on the door. There are two front doors on the caretaker's house—a solid inner door that opens to a small alcove, and a pair of glass doors that open to the porch. From the commotion, it sounded as if someone had broken through the outer doors and was in the alcove trying to break into the house.

Chip called the State Police, and although their headquarters is nearby, he found it strange that they didn't know where the cemetery was, so it was clear that no help would be there anytime soon. Chip ran

87

upstairs to put the baby in her crib, then came back downstairs, determined to face the intruder by himself. Opening the door to the alcove, he was surprised that there wasn't anyone inside, and more surprised that the outer doors were closed and locked. Stepping onto the porch, he didn't see anyone.

The view out the front door where something was banging.

Could the intruder have run away? Not likely, as it was raining heavily, yet there were no wet footprints on the wooden stairs or porch. Perhaps it would be appropriate to say that everything was dry as a bone? Clearly, no human being had walked up to the door and started pounding on it. Then what could it have been? Chip began to wonder if the dead surrounding his house were not quite so dead after all.

Twenty years after that incident, Chip is still caretaker, and the Walkill Cemetery still provides constant reminders that death is not final. Perhaps the activity there is relatively recent, or perhaps this has been a paranormally active location since the cemetery began in the 1700s. Most likely, the spirits have gradually accumulated over the centuries, patiently waiting for people who are sensitive enough to sense their presence.

Walkill Cemetery. The house is down the hill by the road.

Which brings up a curious point—when I interviewed Chip, I asked if he, or anyone else in his family, had any psychic abilities. His immediate answer was no, but over the next hour he related numerous stories that showed that he and just about every relative in his large family has had more than one ghostly encounter. It seems that he and his brother (who is a caretaker at another local cemetery) have both gone into the right profession!

Another early incident involved the carpet in a room at the back of the house that faces the cemetery. Out of the blue one day there appeared to be some kind of dark stain. It wasn't like one of the kids had dropped a glass of soda or had tracked muddy footprints. This discoloration was very much in the shape of a person and the stain actually looked more like a shadow. It was as if someone was standing by the window, arms reaching upward, and the shadow was being cast across the carpet.

Unnerved by its sudden appearance and shape, Chip shampooed the carpet, but the shadow remained. Then he thoroughly cleaned the window inside and out in case dirt was casting that pattern, but still the shadowy figure of a torso, head, and arms remained. Despite all Chip's efforts, the dark pattern didn't change until about four months later when, for no particular reason, it completely disappeared overnight, and it never returned!

I asked Chip if he could possibly determine any characteristics from the size and shape of the Shadow, and after some thought he said it most resembled a figure of a young girl. This is interesting, because the apparition of a girl is perhaps the most common paranormal occurrence on the property.

It began about seven years ago, as Chip was watching a NASCAR race on television. Off to his side, out of the corner of his eye he saw a girl standing there, and assumed it was just one of his daughters wanting something. He really didn't want to be disturbed, but the girl continued to stand there, so finally in frustration he gave up, turned and asked, "What do you want?"

No one was there. No human girl could have disappeared so quickly. Still, he had to check to see if it could possibly have been one of his daughters, but found that none of them had been downstairs. This little girl has been seen on numerous occasions ever since then. Chip's eldest daughter and her friend saw her standing in the driveway, and her friend was so scared by the sight that she refuses to ever come back.

Another time Chip was sitting in the living room and heard and saw a female about five feet tall dressed in white run down the stairs, go through the dining room and head straight for his office. The office door is very noisy, and when he didn't hear the door open, he got up to see what his oldest daughter was up to. The office door was still closed and no one was in the dining room. Checking his office, he found it empty.

Convinced that he had clearly seen an older girl or woman wearing white run through the house, he went upstairs to speak to his daughter. She was sitting quietly in her room, and said she had not been downstairs. Chip didn't doubt her, because not only wasn't she breathing like someone who had just been running quickly, she was wearing a bright red shirt, not a white one.

Who was this short female; a former resident of the house, or a lonely spirit buried in the cemetery? Had she been responsible for the mysterious shadow on the carpet? Was she also responsible for another bizarre burial that occurred?

The house, which may be occupied by more than the living.

One evening Chip went to settle into his favorite chair, and as he lowered himself down, it felt as though he was sitting on someone already in the chair. It was a real, solid feeling, as real as the hands that suddenly pressed against his back, as if someone was pushing him off their lap. Yelling in surprise, he jumped up, searching for some way to explain what had just happened. Nothing visible was on his chair, and he had to face the possibility that he just sat on top of a dead person.

Seeing a figure was one thing; a close encounter like this was something completely different. This spirit had crossed the line, and although it was his favorite chair, he immediately dragged it out onto the porch. The next day he drove it out to a remote section of the cemetery and buried it! Fear will make people do strange things, and I have to admit that this is the first time I've heard of a funeral for a haunted chair.

Perhaps the most unpleasant experiences began several years ago. Chip's now ex-wife, took a Ouija board into his office and began trying to communicate with the spirits. The seemingly harmless experiment took a terrible turn, and it seemed as though she became possessed by the board. It was like she was unable to break free of it, and used it nonstop for several hours that day. She finally was able to tear herself away from the Ouija board, but shortly after a horrible "dead smell" filled the office.

The office where a deathly smell sometimes fills the air.

At first, Chip thought that perhaps something had died in the walls, but when days stretched to months and then years, he realized the smell could not be from any animal as it would have completely decomposed long ago. The awful odor would come and go at any time of the day or season, and would often be so strong that Chip would have to leave his office. And it all began that day his ex-wife became obsessed by the Ouija board. What had she invited into the house through the board, and will it ever leave?

Recently, another man was using his laptop computer in the office when the dead smell began to fill the air. At first he tried to ignore it, but it grew stronger and he finally asked Chip where on earth that horrible stench of death was coming from. Then his laptop began to flicker and flip between different screens, and suddenly the computer inexplicably lost power. It was a very traumatic experience for a skeptic.

On my visit the odor did not make an appearance, but if it's as bad as everyone claims, I can't say that I'm particularly upset that it spared me.

On a more positive spiritual note, Chip's uncle used to tell him that when he died he would come back to haunt his nephew, in a good-natured way, of course. Shortly after his uncle died, Chip was in his bedroom and smelled a very strong odor of grease. He checked the clothes he had worn that day to see if he had gotten some grease or oil on them from any of the cemetery's equipment. The clothes were clean, and he couldn't track down the smell to an object; it seemed to only be in the air. Then he recalled that his uncle was a mechanic, and always smelled of grease. Could this have been his uncle's "calling card" to let his nephew know he had made good on his promise to "haunt" him?

Just in case that relatively subtle message didn't get through, his uncle had one more trick up his post mortem sleeve—he actually made an appearance! One day Chip saw a human figure dressed in black walking across the first floor. Although the features weren't distinct, there was one clear indication that it was indeed his uncle. The figure was sporting a silver bolo tie, exactly like the one his uncle wore (and by the way, the one in which he was buried). Now there wasn't any doubt as to who had come to visit, and having made his point, his uncle's grease smell and apparition never returned.

As if the Walkill Cemetery doesn't have enough real ghosts,

Chip's uncle, who made an appearance—as promised! Note the silver bolo tie.

Chip has hosted Halloween parties during which friends dress up and hide in the cemetery, and jump out to scare the kids on a haunted hayride. Unfortunately, one of the faux ghouls got more than he bargained for as he stood in the darkness in an open gazebo-style mausoleum, waiting for the kids to come by. Someone started pushing him from behind, and the man thought it was Chip trying to scare him, so he did not react at first.

However, the pushing continued, and he finally turned to tell Chip that his little joke wasn't working, but no one was there! Without another moment's hesitation he ran as fast as he could. He later discovered that Chip hadn't been anywhere near that gazebo, and no one else had, either.

The brick gazebo-style mausoleum.

There's another bizarre, but possibly significant, story connected with this mausoleum. In the late 1960s or early 1970s, someone dug up the bodies buried beneath it. The bones were removed from their coffins, and the skulls were placed on sticks. Whether this was done as part of some black magic ritual, or just someone's sick idea of a prank, is not known. Perhaps this terrible desecration has left the spirits on guard for other intruders, and decided to push the poor man in the Halloween costume out of *their* place of eternal rest (which appears to be a relative term in this case).

There have been other incidents on the cemetery grounds, many of which were experienced by Chip's brother when he worked there. Most notably, he often heard voices when no one was around, and sometimes the voices would call his name! He actually became quite paranoid about it, and who can blame him? How would you feel if disembodied voices beckoned you by name in a cemetery? Needless to say, he was quite happy to accept a job offer from another cemetery, where speaking is done only by the living.

Chip is also a volunteer firefighter, and a few of his fellow firefighters were at the house one evening when they all heard the back door open and loudly slam shut. At the time, Chip was going through a divorce and they thought it was his wife angrily entering the house. They all waited, but no one spoke and there weren't any footsteps. The entrance to the basement is by the back door, so Chip assumed she had gone into the basement for some reason, but when he got up to look, he saw that her car wasn't in the driveway. In fact, there weren't any cars other than those of his friends.

Realizing that the door may have been slammed by a dead visitor, the big brave firefighters got spooked, and to a man quickly left the house. Chip asked if any of them would accompany him to the basement to make sure it wasn't a living intruder, but all of the volunteers declined to volunteer this night. Chip searched the basement alone, and did not find anyone, so perhaps leaving had been the smart choice.

Another night Chip and his daughters were watching television in the living room. It was late, and the kids had all fallen asleep. Suddenly, there was loud screaming that didn't seem to be coming from the television. Just to be sure, he muted the sound, and realized the screaming was coming from a woman in his kitchen!

Jumping up, he reached and turned on the living room light, and all at once all three bulbs blew out as if from a surge of electricity. Now he would have to go into the kitchen in total darkness, because the light in there was turned on and off by a string hanging from the middle of the room.

Imagine the scene—you have your three daughters with you, the lights have blown out, and an unknown woman is screaming in terror in the next room. It was the last thing he wanted to do, but Chip took a deep breath, ran full speed into the kitchen, and yanked on the light. The screaming instantly stopped, and no one was there. Fortunately, this was the one and only time this occurred, and like many other of the strange events here, there appears to be no explanation for it.

The kitchen, where a phantom woman screams.

The most recent event happened just a few days before I arrived. Once again, Chip was in the living room, this time sleeping peacefully on the couch. Suddenly there was a tremendous crashing sound in the kitchen that made him practically leap out of his skin. It sounded as if someone had picked up one of the heavy wooden stools and smashed it on the floor. In a heartbeat he was in the kitchen, but not a single thing was out of place or disturbed.

When I interviewed Chip and his family it was a hot, sunny afternoon. The cemetery is in a beautiful location and there certainly didn't seem to be anything spooky about it. Of course, rule number one of ghost hunting—looks can be deceiving.

Chip and I walked the grounds and he pointed out places where strange things had happened. We also went into the receiving building where bodies are stored in their caskets as they await their burial. Many inexplicable things have occurred here to Chip and other employees, and he had even found EMF readings with a meter he had recently purchased. As the building does not have any electricity, there should be no reason for any measurable electromagnetic field.

The building where bodies are stored prior to burial.

I had my meters with me and sure enough, there were some sizable readings in two places. In the first area stood the racks where the caskets are placed. The strongest reading, however, was around the frame that is placed over the open grave, from which the casket is then lowered into eternal darkness. Bodies spend their last moments above ground in this frame, and loved ones have their last glimpses on earth of the resting place of the departed.

Perhaps there aren't actually ghosts connected to this frame and rack, perhaps it is more of the collected energies of love and grief that charge them? In any event, this is not a happy building, and it was nice to leave its cold, unnerving atmosphere and get back into the warm sunlight.

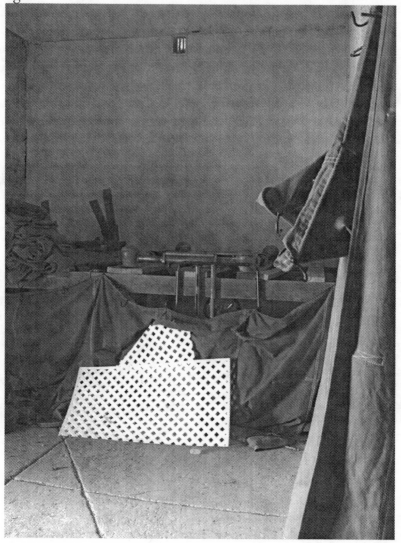

The frame from which the casket is lowered into the grave.

The racks where the caskets are stored.

Apart from the obvious at this cemetery, are there any other possible causes for the numerous hauntings at the Walkill Cemetery? A mill stood on the property in the 1700s, and there is a story that someone was hung there during the Revolution. For many years, an inn was just across the street, but little is known about it. As for the caretaker's house itself, a man died in the kitchen, but the predominant spirits appear to be female.

I think this is a case where history, death, and a very sensitive family have all aligned to create the perfect haunting. Just as an artistic person is best suited to work in a museum, so these people have gravitated to cemeteries. While it is always unsettling and often frightening to have these encounters, it would be nice to think that the dead get some comfort out of being acknowledged again by Chip and his family. Hopefully, the majority of these spirits just come and go one final time before moving on to something better.

It is all something we will each face one way or the other someday, so why not take a lesson from these encounters and live the best life you can now, so you won't need to bother the living from your grave...

# Village of Spirits
## Haverstraw, NY

During the summer of 2007, I was contacted by reporter Robert Zeliger of *Rockland Magazine*. He wanted to write an article about my book *Ghosts of Rockland County*, and was hoping to go on an actual ghost hunt to see what it's all about. I suggested a few places we could visit, but when he asked if there was somewhere I wanted to go where I had never been before, a light went off.

During the past decade, the number one location which people have asked me about is Letchworth Village, the former mental institution established in 1908, which stretched over 2,000 acres across the towns of Haverstraw and Stony Point, New York. It seemed as though I couldn't give a lecture in the area without someone telling me a personal account of weird happenings in the abandoned buildings. I also had several people who had worked there tell me about some rather awful things that happened to patients, such as abuse, but that was limited to a few employees rather than being a widespread problem.

In any event, when Robert asked if there was that one place I would like to investigate, I didn't hesitate to say Letchworth. However, I just as quickly pointed out that many people over the years had tried to get permission to go into the buildings, all to no avail. And the clock was ticking, as many buildings are slated for demolition to make way for a senior housing project. I was quite surprised, therefore, when just a few days later Robert called to say he had obtained permission. Never underestimate the power of a persistent journalist!

We arranged to meet someone from the town at Letchworth at noon on a warm, sunny August day. When that person didn't show up, a few more phone calls finally brought someone else—let's call him Joe—with a large set of keys. The buildings are constantly being broken into, and locks have been changed several times. What that translated into for us was many keys, both labeled and unlabeled, that would all have to be tried. We walked over to an administration building and Joe began the tedious process of trying to open the lock.

Apparently the labels, and most of the keys, were obsolete, and when he exhausted every possibility on one door we went to the next door, and then the next with no luck. We were clearly getting nowhere fast, so I suggested trying another building that may have easier access, such as the one we found with the door kicked in.

One of the many overgrown abandoned buildings.

(*A point of warning here—DO NOT trespass into these buildings! In addition to the danger of hurting yourself, there has been gang activity in these buildings. There may also be other unsavory characters that could pose a threat. The police are always on patrol in the area, as well, and you will be arrested for trespassing. You can drive through or walk the grounds during the day if you want to see the place, but no ghost hunt is worth getting hurt or arrested, so stay away at night! )

Entering through the broken door, we found what looked to be a series of offices. Many of the ceiling tiles had collapsed onto the moldy carpeting, decaying office furniture, smashed telephones, and bits of shattered glass. Graffiti covered almost every wall, and beer cans and cigarette butts were prevalent, speaking to both the frequent and recent intrusions of partiers. Even in the bright sunlight, much of the interior was in darkness, and we needed our flashlights to safely navigate through the unpleasantly fragrant debris.

There wasn't any electricity running to the building, so there should not have been any significant EMF readings. However, I did come across one small area where my digital EMF meter measured

Reporter Robert Zeliger takes notes in the room where there were high EMF readings (back near the door). Below, the area by the bucket was where the sounds originated.

substantial energy that came and went several times. We all stood quietly in that room, and when I asked for some sign there was a clear noise about fifteen feet away. However, Joe had been standing near that spot a few minutes earlier, so we could not rule out the possibility that some debris was settling after having been disturbed by his feet. Of course, we also couldn't say that it wasn't a sound generated in response to my request.

The basement was basically composed of two big open rooms, with several smaller rooms near the door. We were in the large room at the far end and I was using my digital camera in the infrared mode. To my left, I saw a small light moving about fifteen feet away. I reached for my camcorder so I could record the movement, but it was gone by the time the camcorder came on.

I walked over to the spot where the light had appeared, and found significant EMF readings. Robert came over and we both felt an icy chill. I know this isn't measurable proof, but for the first time since entering Letchworth I felt as though something, or more accurately someone, was there. The cold and EMF readings persisted and I would have liked to have set up more cameras and equipment in this area. Unfortunately, our time was limited and we had to move on.

The area where there was a moving light, cold spot and high EMF.
(Infrared image.)

So many haunted buildings, so little time...

On our way out of the basement, my attention was drawn to a small, windowless room with a heavy, rusted metal door. The door wouldn't budge, but it was open just wide enough for me to squeeze through. A few seconds after entering the room, I heard the most unnerving sound and it had originated very close to me, somewhere in the darkness. It was like a choked or gagging cry. It was loud, and seemed to be no more than a foot or two away from me.

Joe was in the hall with the camcorder and I asked if he had heard the sound. Coming closer to the door, he said he hadn't heard anything, but a moment later the bizarre human-like sound was back, even louder and closer. You know the way some people react when someone scrapes a blackboard with their fingernails? Well, that's how I felt as a chill shot up my spine at the awful, tormented cry. This time Joe heard it loud and clear, and it is a sound neither of us will soon forget. He described it as a "gargling sound," and indeed it did resemble the sound of liquid in the throat, but not in a benign way. This was like someone choking, or dare I even say being strangled.

We waited quietly and anxiously for the sound to return, but it did not, and at that point I can't say that I was disappointed. Can you imagine being in a small, dark, windowless room in the basement of a former mental institution hearing what sounds like someone being strangled right next to you? It sure felt good to get out of that basement and into the warm sunlight again!

Our next stop was an eerie and imposing structure, the dilapidated hospital. There is a cemetery on the outskirts of Letchworth Village with the simple graves of over 850 children and adults, and another cemetery with over 500 graves, and it is likely that many of these unfortunate people lost there lives in this hospital. What pain and suffering did these crumbling walls witness?

The building is clearly a popular place to break into and vandalize. The graffiti speaks to the mentality and ignorance of these people with derogatory references to "retarts." I think these people ought to spend more time in school and less time trespassing.

The sprawling hospital has two wings stretching back behind the main building. We carefully made our way down debris covered hallways and found the staircase to the basement. It was very dark, but we found our way to a room that still contained a hospital bed. There were some tantalizing EMF readings here, so I decided to place my Tri-Field meter on the bed.

104

As we stood there quietly, the meter began to squeal lightly, then more loudly and persistently. It would settle down for a few moments, then go off again. Even after turning down the sensitivity, the meter continued to detect an EM field that grew in strength, faded, then returned again and again. I have no explanation for it, given that we were in a building with no natural electrical source.

After further exploration of the basement, we came across the morgue. This would be the one spot where you might expect some activity, but there wasn't anything detected by the meters or cameras. However, while nothing paranormal took place, I do want to point out that something at least abnormal had previously occurred. The individual morgue doors and the autopsy table have all been stolen. I know some people think I'm weird for what I do, but come on, taking home morgue doors and an autopsy table? That's just sick.

We found some labs that must have once been bustling with activity and stocked with high tech equipment and all manner of potent medications. Now dark and empty, there's little more to see than paint peeling off of walls and weeds growing in through the broken windows. Having worked in a lab for many years (I was a research chemist at a medical diagnostics company), I found this to be a particularly unsettling sight. It was a stark reminder that nothing lasts,

The morgue. The individual wooden doors have been removed.

and things that seem important today will be crumbling to dust all too soon.

I suppose the depressing surroundings were just starting to get to me. It was hard not to imagine the spirits of many, many children in little hospital gowns wandering these gloomy, godforsaken corridors. I had learned that the graves of these poor "inmates" only had numbers, not names, as relatives did not want the "shame" of having it known that there had been a mentally handicapped child in the family. It was painfully sad to realize that these children had been abandoned and forgotten in life, and now would be eternally forgotten in death.

Will demolishing these buildings release the energies that may be trapped within these walls? One could only hope, but more often than not, spirits tend to linger to haunt the new structures built over the site of their suffering.

Time will tell. But time is running out for the crumbling buildings of Letchworth Village. Perhaps some day, like the patients it housed for decades, it too will be forgotten...

A hallway in the hospital.

# Darker Forces
## Orange County, NY

The owner of the house in the story on page 14 was speaking with an acquaintance one day and mentioned the strange activity that was connected to a suicide. To his astonishment, the other man, "Jack," told him that there had also been a suicide in his nephew's house, and that there has recently been paranormal activity. In addition to having similar experiences, these two cases shared something else in common—the same street! It's unusual enough to live on a road where someone has shot himself to death and now haunts the place, but can you imagine two such cases with practically the same address?

I contacted Jack, and then his nephew, "Steve," and after hearing their stories decided that I had to investigate this house as soon as possible. Based upon my prior knowledge of this area, I knew that it was prone to unusual energies, but I had no idea to what extent until that night. It was as surprising as it was disturbing, and as I write this less than twelve hours after the investigation, the effects are still with me, and not in a particularly good way...

The house was built in 1959, coincidentally, by the grandfather of the Steve's girlfriend, "Laura." The household consisted of Jack, his brother, "Gary," their parents and their grandfather, "Hank." There was considerable friction in the house, mostly due to the fact that Hank was an alcoholic, and not a friendly one, either. It had reached a point where Hank was going to have to go, but before they could send him packing, he took matters into his own hands.

One early July evening in 1971, Hank was in his room, while most of the family and a friend were relaxing in the yard after dinner. Jack's mother was in the kitchen washing dishes. Suddenly there was a sharp, loud "BANG," and the ever-concerned mother called outside to see if the kids were playing with firecrackers. Everyone outside agreed that it sounded like the explosive noise had come from inside the house. There was an awful moment of realization, and in instant everyone started running for Hank's room.

They found Hank slumping over on his bed, the .38 Special still clutched in his hand.

"Hank, what did you do?" Jack's father shouted.

Nasty until the end, Hank swore at his son-in-law with his final words. He had no vital signs in the ambulance on the way to the hospital, where he was pronounced D.O.A.

While the domestic situation remained turbulent even after Hank's suicide, there wasn't any particular paranormal activity that the family noticed. In 1992, Jack's mother suffered a stroke and passed away in the hospital. In 2000, Jack's father became seriously ill and wanted to die in the house he loved so much. A bed was set up in the living room, and family, friends, and hospice workers took care of him until the end. Although he slipped into a deep coma in his bed, he did not actually die until he was brought to the hospital.

At this point, Jack and Gary decided to keep the house in the family and sell it to Gary's son, Steve. Although sadness and tragedy had tainted the place's past, it seemed to have a bright future with Steve and his girlfriend. However, soon after moving in, his girlfriend began complaining of a male presence. Steve works nights, and incidents only seemed to occur when he was out of the house. Or so he thought.

Steve would constantly find the refrigerator door open, and a row of lights in the basement recreation room would be on, even after he was certain he had turned them off. Repeatedly asking his girlfriend if she was responsible for the refrigerator door and the lights, she would invariably reply that she always shut the door tightly, and usually hadn't even been in the basement on the days the lights were found on. (By the way, that row of lights is operated by two separate switches at opposite ends of the room, so they could not both be turned on by accident.) It was hard to believe that she was not responsible. After all, what other explanation could there be?

After that relationship ended and she moved out, the lights still continued to go on and the refrigerator door continued to be found open, so Steve realized she had indeed been telling the truth. When his new girlfriend moved in, she also felt a male presence. She told Steve that her parents' house was also haunted, and that she was sensitive to spirits. No one quite believed her, even after she insisted that someone had physically touched her hair, and that one night when she was in the hallway she saw an old man in the kitchen.

With more of the intent to prove that she was making up the story, Gary asked, "Okay then, what did this old man look like?"

To everyone's amazement, she went on to describe a bald man wearing wire-rimmed glasses, and other characteristics that fit Hank to a T. She had never seen a picture of him, so could not have known these details. No one ever scoffed at her again.

Looking down the hall to the kitchen, where Steve's girlfriend saw an old man standing.

When that relationship ended, it was out with girlfriend number two, and in with Laura, girlfriend number three (don't worry, the list stops here, for now). Laura has also had a remarkable encounter, which took place at 4am. She gets up very early for work, and one morning when she went into the kitchen to get some coffee, she distinctly heard an old man's voice in the room with her. She couldn't make out any words as it was more of a mumbling or muffled voice, but she has no doubt what she heard.

This is not only interesting of itself, but especially in lieu of what happened to Mike soon after he, Bob, and I arrived the night of the investigation. We all gathered in the living room so I could conduct the interviews, and Mike stood by the kitchen doorway. Soon after we began, he heard a "muffled man's voice" in the kitchen. It was at least a sentence or two, but he couldn't make out any words. Thinking it was another family member, he turned to see who was speaking, but didn't see anyone. In fact, no one else was in the house. He didn't think anymore about it until Laura told her story of the old man's mumbling voice in the kitchen.

There were other revelations during the interviews. After Steve finished describing the numerous incidents with the refrigerator door, Jack recalled that decades ago this had been one of Hank's irritating habits. After coming home late from a night of heavy drinking he would rummage through the refrigerator for something to eat, and in his stupor he would often forget to close the door!

There was even more amazing information revealed by Gary, something I didn't know before, and something Steve had just recently found out, as well—much to his dismay. Back in the early 1960s, a boy who lived just three houses away decided to play a trick on his sister. He dug a hole in the backyard where he knew she would be passing, and then thought it was quite funny when she fell in.

However, no one was laughing when the boy's father came to rescue his daughter, and found a skull and bones in the hole with the little girl. She had fallen into an ancient grave!

The state brought in a team of archaeologists who roped off the area and told all of the kids to stay out. One by one, they exhumed remains from a large Indian burial ground. No one was quite sure just how extensive it was, however, because one day the archaeologists just stopped digging and left. Perhaps their funding ran out, or perhaps there were other untold reasons?

In any event, all you need to do is tell kids to stay away from something and they are drawn to it like moths to a flame. Even though an archaeologist told Gary that if he took anything from the graves the Indian spirits would "come and get you," he couldn't resist taking some beads he found. Rushing home with his stolen funereal treasure, he put them in a white envelope and hid them on top of the ductwork in the basement for fear of being caught.

The thought that he had stolen something from an Indian burial ground continued to haunt him, but years later when he went to retrieve the beads they were gone, and have never been found! He hadn't told anyone about them, and certainly no one had any reason to be poking around the top of the basement heating ducts.

So, this house had been built on the edge—if not directly on top of—a genuine Indian burial ground, and Gary had brought home artifacts from a grave. Could any of this have some bearing on the haunted activity? Did anyone ever experience anything unusual in that basement?

Yes, and yes! And I can say that from personal experience!

It's not unusual for kids to be scared of their basements. They're often dark, dusty, and full of spiders and other crawling creatures. However, in this house the majority of the basement is a finished recreation room with a full-sized bar. This was always a place of fun and parties. Just a small section of the basement is unfinished, but it is clean and well lit. The only problem was getting to the light switch…

The switch for the bright fluorescent light fixture is in the back corner of the room. Jack and Gary always felt this area was "very creepy" and had often asked their father to move the switch closer to the doorway. Steve felt the same way, yet no one had actually ever heard or seen anything unusual, until a few months ago.

That back corner has a long workbench, and one night Steve was busy with a project. To his right, out of the corner of his eye, he thought he saw a shadow. Turning, he saw a tall, dark figure move quickly across the room and disappear into the wall near the "creepy" corner. Though mostly shadowy and indistinct with only a shoulder and one arm well defined, it did appear to be a muscular male over six feet tall. It was there and gone in a second or two, but there was no doubt that something had been in that basement room with him and had gone right through the wall.

Before I describe our experiences from that night, let me back up and start at the beginning of the evening. After the interviews, we started getting our equipment ready. I decided to take a quick check of the suicide bedroom with my EMF meter. I repeatedly got high readings just in one spot, and asked Steve if any of the audio equipment stored in the room might be on, thereby producing the readings. The only thing that was plugged in was the fax machine, and that was on the other side of the room.

I decided to put the more sensitive Tri-field meter on the spot where Hank shot himself. This meter has a needle indicator and an audible alarm, so you know from a distance if there is a detectable EM field. My plan was to set up a camcorder in the room aimed at the meter, but while we were still getting the equipment ready in the living room I thought I heard something. The family had gone outside, so I knew no one else was in the house.

I went to Hank's room with my camcorder and found that the meter was buzzing softly, which indicated there was now a low but steady EM field around the meter, which was not there a few minutes earlier. I started my camcorder and pointed it at the meter. The readings persisted and after a minute I asked, "Is there someone who wants to make his presence known?"

The needle moved and the buzzing grew louder for an instant, meaning the field had briefly increased as if in response to my question. Then I asked, "Is it Grandpa Hank?"

The meter sounded even more loudly this time, and I knew this was more than a coincidence. I called to Bob and Mike and suggested we all sit in the room to see what else would happen, but after they arrived, the meter became silent and nothing else occurred. Hank had previously only made his presence known to women, was he continuing the trend during this investigation?

I did have the distinct impression that I would get more results that night if I was by myself, but I didn't realize the full impact that would have on me. I was also still under the assumption that this haunting was all about Hank, with perhaps a few minor residual energies hanging around. In other words, I was completely surprised by what was about to happen.

Mike had set up a camcorder in the unfinished basement room, and as is our usual practice we left the basement to make sure that whatever the camcorder heard or saw had nothing to do with the living. Our plan was to stay out of the basement for a while, but I began to feel compelled to go down there alone. The feeling grew stronger until

I couldn't resist the impulse to find out why. I told Bob and Mike that I needed to go into the basement by myself.

"I don't like the idea, but I feel I have to go alone," I added.

With my camcorder running, I began to descend the dark basement stairs. As I reached the bottom, I heard a sound to my right in the unfinished section, something like shuffling footsteps. I called upstairs to tell them what I heard. A moment later there was a soft tapping sound directly in front of me on, or in, the wall. Undaunted, I continued into the rec room section.

Taping in infrared, I slowly scanned the length of the room. Something caught my eye in the viewfinder—one of those little white specs that often go whizzing by, and are usually nothing more that dust or other airborne particles reflecting the infrared light. This one was a little different. It moved slowly, and almost deliberately, diagonally through the air and disappeared near a rocking chair. I made a mental note of it, and moved on.

Later, when I told the family what I had found, I mentioned the moving white spot and it turned out that the rocking chair used to be in the living room and it was where Hank always sat! I suppose it still could have been a piece of dust, but it would be quite a coincidence that the only such spot I witnessed all night just happened to direct my attention to the one piece of furniture in the basement connected most closely to Hank.

When nothing else occurred in the rec room area, I headed over to the unfinished section. There are two rooms on that side of the basement, and I stood on the threshold between the first smaller room, and the larger workroom where Mike had set up the camcorder, and where Steve had seen the fleeting shadow. Initially, I stood there so I did not get in the line of sight of the camcorder, but after a few moments I felt a distinct difference between the two rooms, and crossing that threshold took on new meaning.

I felt I should turn off my camcorder and other equipment and just stand quietly in the dark. I didn't know what to expect, but in my mind I asked to know what this was all about, why I was compelled to come down to the basement alone, and what forces were at work in this house.

What's that old saying, "Be careful what you ask for?"

Now before I describe what happened, I have to say I feel uncomfortable writing about this entire encounter. In retrospect it sounds like something out of a Hollywood special effects studio, but believe me it was all frightening real. If you know anything about my work, you know I'll always report what I find, or don't find, as clearly and accurately as possible. It's your prerogative to think the following is all nonsense or my imagination, but here it is:

I stood in the doorway facing the back corner (I didn't know at that point they referred to it as the "creepy corner.") I could faintly see the outline of the room from the dim light of Mike's camcorder indicator lights. Once I turned off my equipment, I devoted my full attention to just looking, listening, and feeling. Suddenly, I thought I detected movement from the back corner.

I could not tell you whether I physically saw or psychically envisioned a tall figure emerge from the corner, but it didn't matter either way, as the impact was just as dramatic! There was no fear, just surprise and fascination almost to the point of being entranced. The figure was dark and featureless, but the outline and the impressions that emanated from it made me think it was masculine and Native American.

As if that wasn't amazing enough, what I saw next completely blew my mind. Behind the tall figure emerged two shorter figures, one on either side. Then behind them emerged several more, forming a dark triangle of figures that slowly and deliberately began moving straight toward me. I don't know if there were six or ten or dozens behind them. Now, I admit I was beginning to feeling just a bit alarmed, but that wasn't the half of it.

I didn't hear any sounds with my ears, but somehow I "heard" that they were "many." They weren't evil or malicious, but my blood ran cold as I began to strongly feel that this was not the sort of thing the living should come into contact with, that these were forces of the dead and it would not be healthy—for me!—if we came together.

As the lead figure drew within about four feet from me, my self-preservation instincts all kicked in and I knew I had to get the hell out of there quickly. Even though they didn't threaten me and I had no sense of being attacked, I needed to go before they moved any closer. I didn't scream, I didn't run, but I sure moved swiftly to the staircase, and breathed a deep sigh of relief when I got upstairs. Fortunately, "they" did not follow, although when I sat down on the living room floor, I still sensed that "they" were right underneath me.

Bob and Mike took one look at me and asked what had happened. I must have looked like I had just seen a ghost. One ghost wouldn't have been so bad, "many" was pushing it!

The corner of the basement where dark figures come and go through the wall.

I took a minute to compose myself, and then carefully put into words as best as I could what had just transpired. As I tried to explain the formation of the emerging rows of figures, Mike suggested it was like a pattern of bowling pins, and I realized that was the best description. I stressed that they weren't anything threatening, and it was definitely a case of getting what I asked for. I also explained that I felt as those these energies were from the other world, and should stay there!

After a few minutes, curiosity overcame common sense once again and we all went into the basement. While we didn't hear or see anything, there was an electricity in the air. Even Bob uncharacteristically complained of a tingling sensation repeatedly rising up his spine. And trying to stand for any length of time in the back corner proved to be a very uncomfortable proposition.

As I stood in the room near where the tall figure had stood just a few minutes earlier, I felt myself slipping away for a moment and could picture all the figures in my mind again. Then I got the impression, or "heard," that they searched for souls. When I repeated this out loud to Bob and Mike they looked at each other, then back to me, and we all had a similar expression on our faces—one of alarm.

It all kind of hit us at once—chills up the spine and the overwhelming feeling that even if our minds were playing tricks on us, we had to get out of there. If there was even the remotest chance that these soul-gathering spirits walked this land in search of the dead and dying, we didn't want to have any contact with them—at least not for a very long time!

Before we exited the basement, I also got the sense of layers of paranormal energy in the house. On the first floor, there was the spiritual energy of Hank, a ghost in the classic sense. There was also the residual impression of Jack and Gary's father in the living room, in a spot just above this basement room where his bed had been placed when he was dying. But that all paled in comparison to the powerful energies in the basement and in the ground around the house. Did this layer spread out and cover the entire area? It was certainly possible, and I would even say likely.

We came back upstairs for a while and discussed what was going on. We all agreed that the night had been a complete surprise. We were hoping to gather evidence concerning the man who had committed suicide, and thought the bulk of the activity would be found in the bedroom and kitchen. When we heard the story of the Indian burial ground it was interesting, but it has always seemed like a vastly overused excuse for all kinds of paranormal events.

Now we were faced with the possibility of a new reality—were the events here the cause, *or the result*, of deeper, darker forces at work? Were these same forces also influencing the people at the other suicide house, and possibly every other house in between?

Gary had told us that for many decades there has been evidence of black magic ceremonies in the surrounding hills, things such as offerings and sacrifices. Are these cults and covens also drawn to the strong paranormal energies in this land?

While we pondered these questions, Mike began to look a bit distracted. He explained that he was also feeling compelled to go into the basement alone. Even after all that had happened, he couldn't shake the feeling, so off he went. I did not think it was a good idea, so after he left I sat on the top step of the basement stairs just to be close in case anything happened.

My intentions were just to be ready to offer any assistance; the result was that I inadvertently caught some of the funniest video we've ever gotten at a haunted site. Unfortunately, it would be at Mike's expense.

Like my experience in the basement by myself, Mike began by monitoring instruments and adjusting his audio recorder, but he also felt as though he should just turn off everything and stay quiet. Almost immediately after he did, a strong electric charge shot through his body, unlike anything he had ever felt before. It grew so potent that he couldn't stand it anymore and had to run.

In the darkness and his haste, he knocked into a folding screen at the bottom of the stairs, which proceeded to come crashing down making a tremendous racket. And who was poised at the top of the stairs taping the entire thing? Yes, that would be me.

Mike was visibly shaken, so the first order of business was to make sure he was okay and "debrief" him about his experience. Apparently, the energy had been so strong it was just short of feeling as though he had stuck his finger in a socket.

Once he had time to unwind and we knew he was going to be all right, we started laughing about his somewhat ungraceful retreat, in what looked and sounded like something out of a Bugs Bunny or Roadrunner cartoon. It is definitely right up there with Mike inadvertently taping his own feet as he ran through Eastern State

Penitentiary, and he was just as good-natured about this amusing footage. Hey, you need a sense of humor on ghost hunts because you are bound to be caught doing something less than heroic at some point.

After these disturbing basement experiences, Bob thought to use the EMF meter in the living room above the creepy corner (which also happened to be where the bed had been placed when the father was dying). There were strong readings in that area that could not be explained by natural electrical sources, so perhaps the energies of the basement do seep upward into the house?

Bob measures the EM field on the living room floor.

The last phase of the investigation was to tell everyone about what we had found. Other than the EMF meter in the bedroom and living room, and the video of the moving light in the basement, I stressed that our other findings were of our own impressions, and therefore not verifiable evidence. It's not to say they weren't accurate representations of what is going on there, but as an investigator you have to make the distinction between hard facts and subjective thoughts and feelings. I can believe my experiences to be true, but I can't rightfully expect others to do so.

In the final analysis, however, what we experienced did ring true to everyone who has lived there. More research and investigating must be done, and it would be fascinating to see what might be unearthed in the ground, as well as in the records for the area. It would also be interesting to see if those burial beads can be found, and if the activity is altered if they are removed from the house. (We did take a quick look for the beads, by standing on a chair that turned out to be from a funeral home! Talk about adding fuel to a fire…)

On a final note, a few weeks after our visit, Steve went into the basement, back into the "creepy corner." He was there for only a second or two when a sharp banging sound went off behind him. It was so loud it sounded like a 12-guage shotgun, and Steve spun around expecting to see an armed intruder.

No one was there, but a large box was now on the floor. The box had come off of a stack of boxes, where it had sat undisturbed for months. He had not been near the box when he entered, so he couldn't have knocked into it and made it fall. Steve even tried to reproduce the gunshot sound by repeatedly dropping the box from the same height, but no matter how it fell, it sounded like the dull thud of a cardboard box, not a blast like the one that almost made Steve jump out of his skin!

Steve is now considering selling this house and building another on some property he owns farther north. In this event I have two suggestions: Carefully check the new building site for graves, and let the new owners know there may be more to the house than the MLS sheet indicated.

For better or for worse, we share our world with some powerful and mysterious forces. They may be present for our benefit, and they may be here to feed off of our frailties. Be cautious when dealing with such things, as they may change your life and impact future generations in ways we can't even imagine.

# Castle Tavern
## Greenwood Lake, New York

The Castle Tavern on Greenwood Lake.

There are some really good ghost stories out there, but unfortunately many of them simply have no supporting evidence. While my overall goal is to provide cases with as many facts as possible, I will occasionally say the heck with it—tell the story now, and hope facts emerge at some later date.

Not that this case hasn't had its share of eyewitness accounts (and good ones at that), it's just that the stories behind the haunted activity cannot be backed up with any written records. At least, not yet. Perhaps someday, someone will hear about this case and produce the paranormal smoking gun in the form of newspaper clippings, diary entries, etc.

For now, here's the tale of lust, revenge, attempted murder, and death that surrounds the Castle Tavern on beautiful Greenwood Lake.

At some point, perhaps the early 1900s, the owner began having an affair with one of the waitresses. This wouldn't have been a particularly bad thing, except that the owner also had a wife, and she wasn't too happy when she found out about her competition.

One day in a jealous rage, the spurned wife set fire to the place in hopes of killing her husband and his mistress. Whether or not she planned to also die in the flames will never be known, but it certainly ended up that way. While some versions of the story differ at this point, the most popular version holds that the husband managed to rescue his mistress, but left his wife to perish in the flames she had created. There are also versions that all three died, but in any case, the traumatic events would have made the Castle Tavern a place ripe for a haunting.

In yet another bizarre twist to this tragic tale—two life-sized paintings that now hang on separate walls in the upstairs dining room are allegedly of the wife and the mistress. Legend has it that the paintings must be kept apart. If they are ever placed side by side, "all hell breaks loose."

In support of this legend is an incident in the recent past when the two painting were taken from the walls and placed together while work was being done on the place. Windows in the room then proceeded to shatter without any discernable cause. It does make for a great story, but I am somewhat skeptical about these paintings of the two women.

At first they appeared to represent European peasant women, rather than early twentieth century Americans, but the stone archways do resemble the architecture of the tavern. Perhaps the arches can be identified by looking more closely throughout the building, or examining old photos if they can be found. Of course, it would also be unusual for someone to commission similar paintings of his wife and mistress, but I guess stranger things have happened.

It is possible that the paintings may be from an art dealer who ran the place as a gallery in the 1940s, and that they are unrelated to the wife and mistress. However, I would love to discover that they are the two lovely points of a former owner's love triangle, as haunted paintings that cannot be put close to one another makes for an awfully good ghost story. If only there were photographs of the past owners to compare with the paintings, or any documents identifying the subjects.

Another strange occurrence also involved paintings at the Castle Tavern. A previous owner had placed several paintings in a storeroom. Years later when they were unrolled, all of them had turned white! I suppose some could argue that exposure to some kind of solvent could have affected the pigments, but I don't think that even dipping a rolled up painting in turpentine would do anything but make the colors run, not turn white.

The painting of the wife?

The painting of the mistress?

Other unsubstantiated rumors about the tavern include Satanic rituals that were conducted during the 1960s or 70s. There is also a story of a boy allegedly falling from a window and dying. While as of yet there isn't any proof to back up these stories, one very real and well documented story did take place here, or at least in the water and on the beach behind the tavern.

In July of 2001, there was a terrible boating accident just offshore of the Castle Tavern. A former waitress at the tavern had returned with five friends for dinner. When they had finished, they got into a boat docked outside and headed onto the lake. A few brief heartbeats later their boat collided with another boat carrying two people. The resulting high-speed collision left four people dead, including the former waitress, and two badly injured. Staff and patrons were horrified as the dead and injured were placed on the beach in front of the restaurant. There is no haunted activity that can be tied directly to this incident, but certainly such a tragedy could leave an impression on the property.

The beach next to the tavern.

The best evidence for ghosts at the Castle Tavern comes from eyewitness accounts, which have been both diverse and numerous. They also occur at any time of the day or night and during any part of the year. There was the girl who was skating on the lake one winter just behind the tavern. The place was closed for the season, but when the girl looked up at the windows, she clearly saw a woman waving to her.

Upon checking, she found that the building was closed and locked up tight, so no one could have been inside.

The upstairs dining room where much of the activity takes place.

Then there was the teenaged boy who worked the grill. One night he helped the owner turn off all the lights and lock up. Shortly after, he remembered he had left something he needed inside and hurried back to see if perhaps the owner was still in the parking lot so that he could retrieve it. The owner had gone, there were no cars in the parking lot, but lights were back on in the upper dining area.

Suddenly "weird music" began to play, the strangest music he had ever heard, unlike anything he had ever heard before or since. It only lasted for a short time, then there was "dead silence" and the lights went out again. The doors were still locked, and the boy had been certain no one was inside when they closed up. There was only one thing he could do when confronted with the lights and unnerving music—run!

The son of a former owner also told me about odd things happening after closing. The normal routine was to blow out all the candles on the tables, double check that the place was dark, and then lock up. However, one night when they got outside, they noticed light coming from the upstairs dining room. Going back in, they found several of the candles were burning again.

Of course, it's possible that once in a while a candle can rekindle its flame if it isn't fully extinguished, but so many of them, and all on the same night? After this happened the first time they made certain the candles were completely out, but the mysterious re-lightning occurred on several other occasions.

A few things of note have happened since the latest owners took over in May of 2006. A customer had too much to drink at a Halloween party, so he was allowed to stay and sleep on a couch in the dining area. Around 4:30am, he was awakened by an old cleaning lady who abruptly told him he had to leave immediately. He said he would go, then promptly turned over and went back to sleep for a few more hours.

The next day he told Tony (one of the current owners) that the old cleaning lady tried to get him out of the restaurant in the middle of the night. This was very surprising—not because of the rude behavior of the cleaning lady, but because they had no cleaning lady! No one else was in the restaurant that night.

Now I know that since alcohol was involved this is not the best eyewitness testimony, and I wouldn't have even mentioned the episode, except for the fact that similar experiences have occurred involving this couch and an old lady.

One night Tony and his wife, Dawn, were too tired to go home after a long day. They decided to sleep on the large couch. Around 4am, they each had a "scary dream" about an old lady. When they compared notes the next day, their descriptions of the lady were identical, as was the frightening feelings they experienced during their dreams. Tony assured me that he never has bad dreams that he can recall, but this one he remembers in vivid detail because it seemed so real.

Is there something about this couch or the spot it was in? Or is it simply the case that one of the spirits does not like people intruding in her territory late at night?

Dawn was also involved in what I consider to be the most compelling evidence for paranormal activity at the Castle Tavern. One night when only she and Tony were in the building, she went into the kitchen. At the far end of the kitchen is a small storeroom, and she saw someone move quickly across the room from right to left. The figure was something of a blur, but it appeared to be almost black at the top and bottom, but seemed to have a bright reddish color in the middle.

It was odd looking, but as she only glimpsed it for a second, Dawn just assumed it was Tony. She waited a minute for him to speak or emerge from the storeroom, but there was only silence.

"Tony, don't you jump out at me!" Dawn said, thinking her husband was trying to play a joke and frighten her.

Still there was silence, and she was becoming genuinely scared. Cautiously, she moved closer to the room, still thinking—and perhaps by this point, hoping—that the figure she had seen was Tony, but when she reached the room it was empty, and there was no other way out.

Shortly after, she found Tony working downstairs. Dawn asked if he had just been up in the kitchen, and he replied that he had been downstairs the entire time. There was simply no explanation for the dark figure in the storeroom. That was not to be the last time this figure appeared, either.

Dawn had not mentioned the incident to her sister, who shortly after came to work at the tavern. One evening as the two women tended the bar, Dawn asked her sister to get some more chips from the kitchen. A minute later her sister returned looking very pale and frightened.

"I can't work here," she told her sister. When asked why, she replied, "I saw something."

Dawn was thinking that perhaps she had seen a bug or a mouse, but that was not the case. When her sister had entered the kitchen, she saw a frightening figure move across the store room, going from right to left. It was something of a blur, but she could clearly see colors of red, orange, and yellow. She had no idea what it was, but one thing was for certain—she never wanted to see anything like it again.

This is pure speculation on my part, but as Dawn was explaining to me what she and her sister had seen, I couldn't help but think that it was probably similar to what a person engulfed in flames would look like as he or she ran in panic. Was this entity trying to get its message across in the colors of fire? As I said, it's pure speculation, but something to keep in mind. Obviously, there is something in that storeroom trying to make its presence known, and has chosen a very unique method for doing so.

There have been quite a few other incidents that are odd, but could possibly be explained by faulty plumbing, such as faucets turning

The storeroom at the end of the kitchen.

on by themselves, or toilets flushing when no one was near them. However, harder to explain was an air conditioner that suddenly turned on in the middle of the winter in front of several eyewitnesses. The unit is mounted in the wall near the ceiling, and the controls can only be reached by standing on a ladder, so it could not have been turned on accidentally.

The most recent episodes are also among the most dramatic, or at the least, the most energetic. There are heavy glass candle holders in the bar area, and one evening a candle holder suddenly flew off a shelf and traveled many feet in the air before hitting the floor. The bartender and several amazed customers witnessed the event, as did a security camera! The footage shows that no one was anywhere near the candle holder as it was inexplicably launched into the air as if someone had thrown it.

Just a week before I arrived there was a similar incident. Again, in front of startled witnesses, a large shell came out of a display shelf, went through the air at least ten feet, then smashed on the floor. No one was near the shelf at the time, and even if someone had bumped into it, the displaced shell would not have had the energy to travel so far through the air.

I think the Castle Tavern has many secrets. Often, there is some basis of fact to stories and rumors, especially those as widespread and dramatic as a spurned wife setting fire to the place. There is unquestionably paranormal activity here, and some tragedies or unfulfilled desires must be behind them.

People are always asking me where they can go to experience the supernatural firsthand, and haunted restaurants are a great place to check the degree of your sixth sense. I definitely recommend you try this place, and perhaps you will be the one to find that evidence of the tavern's shaded past, or get a message from one of the spirits that try to communicate with the living. Even if nothing happens at the Castle Tavern on Greenwood Lake while you're there, you will be certain to have an excellent meal in one the most beautiful settings in the area.

The Castle Tavern does have many secrets. Can you help solve them?

"X" marks the spots where the shell sat on the shelf on the wall, and the location on the floor where the shell landed.

# A Haunted Life

Early in 2007, I was contacted by Ida, a woman who has had a life full of ghostly encounters. It may come as a surprise to some that she is not the first person I've met who has had multiple paranormal experiences at many different locations over the course of several decades.

There are many people out there who begin to doubt their own sanity because it seems that wherever they go they end up living in a haunted house. There could be several reasons for this:

- They are very sensitive and are unconsciously drawn to places with paranormal activity.
- Spirits are everywhere; it's just a question of the level of awareness by the occupants.
- Ghosts are drawn to them because they know they can successfully make their presence known.
- They just have really, really bad luck.

It is most likely some combination of all of the above, and I think it's important to make people in this situation aware that they are not alone. It is equally important to realize that for these people, what the average person considers to be unusual is just a common occurrence to them. The bottom line is this—what is paranormal for some is normal for others.

Here's two perfect examples: Just a couple of weeks before Ida emailed me some of her stories, I was in a store that I hadn't been in before (in Monroe, NY) and just happened to start talking to a woman who worked there. She told me about a nearby pizza place, commenting that the pizza there was good, but another place in town was even better. A few days later I tried their pizza and found that it was better, and resolved that someday I would go back to that store and thank the woman for the recommendation.

Then I got Ida's email, in which she mentioned where she works. A little light went on in my head and I just knew she was the same woman I spoke to, which she later confirmed. Also, it was not the first time we had unknowingly met—she mentioned a house where she used to live just a couple of miles from mine, and I recalled having stopped at a yard sale there several years ago.

Coincidence you say? Perhaps, but explain this one: I had told Ida I would drop by the store to speak to her and get more details on the stories, but things got hectic and weeks turned to months. One day my schedule unexpectedly changed and I had a few spare hours, so I decided to call her at the store and see if I could come by. She answered the phone, and when I identified myself, the tone of her voice was very odd. I went to see her later that afternoon, and she explained why she had sounded so funny.

About 60 seconds before I called, Ida saw a woman who looked like me in the store, and thought, "Oh, Linda has come to see me." However, before she could go and greet the woman the phone rang, and it was me. Remember, this is after several months with absolutely no communication, so she had no idea when, or if, I would actually show up.

As for me, I get this all the time. I wish I had a dollar for every time I called someone and they practically start screaming that they can't believe I just called, because they were just thinking of me, or had my phone number in their hand and were just about to call me. Trust me, this is way beyond coincidence, but is it paranormal? I don't think so. I think we all have the ability to be on the same "wavelength," it's just a matter of not gumming up your circuits with bad habits, and paying attention to such things when they happen. People don't have enough faith in their natural abilities in the realm of the sixth sense.

So, without further ado, I would like to present several of Ida's fascinating experiences as she related them to me, with the understanding that I have not personally investigated any of these sites, although I have been to two of the locations. They are not in chronological order, but have all occurred within the last twenty years. Also, as is often the case, I am not giving the exact locations, as the current business and home owners would most likely not be pleased.


Ida and her friend, Colleen, rented an apartment on the second floor of a house on Piaget Avenue in Clifton, New Jersey. At the time, Colleen worked in Manhattan, and Ida had an antiques shop a few blocks from their apartment. Only a day after moving in, the first awful incident occurred.

Ida was alone in the house, or so she thought, when she began hearing yelling coming from the basement, which could be accessed from a door in the kitchen on the second floor. She knew that the other tenants on the first floor were not home, so she was very concerned that someone had broken into the basement. Cautiously, she opened the door of her apartment and stuck out her head. Instantly, a very angry female voice yelled, "Get out! Get the hell out, both of you!"

Frightened, Ida started to go downstairs, but felt "something very bad" and hurried back up to the second floor. The phone was in the kitchen, near the door to the basement, and she called Colleen to tell her what was happening. As she spoke, the knob on the basement door began rattling violently. It was so loud that Colleen could hear it over the phone, and she begged Ida to leave the house immediately.

Although admittedly scared, Ida also felt her stubborn side, and she wasn't about to let something dead drive her out of her new home. Kicking back at the door, she began screaming, "Leave us alone!" And just in case that didn't work, she put her back against the wall and braced her leg against the door in an attempt to keep the angry female spirit from getting to her.

Whether it was the kicking or screaming, or both, the knob stopped rattling and there wasn't anymore shouting that day—from the living or the dead. In fact, although the activity continued, it was of a totally different nature.

About a week later, Colleen woke up to find an apparition of a woman leaning over her. The woman had an upswept "Gibson girl" hairstyle, and a high-collared dress. She didn't feel any fear, and without physically hearing anything, she "heard" the name Jean. Then the figure disappeared. From that day, Jean was a constant, friendly presence in the apartment.

Another constant was the activity in the attic above them. There were always footsteps and creaking sounds as if someone was using the old rocking chair stored there. At first, they would go up to see who was making the sounds, but when it became clear that no one was visible, they gave up and accepted it.

However, one day they had some friends over, and one of the men asked who kept walking around upstairs. They told him it was probably just Jean, the resident ghost, and being a complete skeptic, he was determined to catch whoever was playing this joke on them, as they were clearly human footsteps. When he returned from the attic, his expression and attitude were quite different, as he found no one.

While there are many questions that remain unanswered, like Jean's identity and why she is there, the most important issue that is still on Ida's mind is this—Was Jean responsible for all of the activity in the house, showing something of a Jekyl and Hyde nature, or had she somehow kept the angry female presence at bay? It's difficult enough to figure out human nature and relationships, so I won't even venture to speculate what goes on in the other world!

---

There is a lovely church over one hundred years old in southern Orange County, New York, that may have a rather dark side to it. For several years Ida worked as a housekeeper in the pastor's house on the property, and she was not alone in having unpleasant experiences in the church. Over the years, many witnesses have reported seeing the ghost of a little boy and a clergyman. There have also been numerous reports of feelings of an evil presence.

One of the worst spots is the corner behind the baptismal font near an old elevator shaft. Ida and others who cleaned the church would always save that area for last, because they always had such horrible feelings, as if something very bad didn't want them there. Similar feelings were experienced in a long hallway and bathroom beneath the church. Ida and a co-worker would literally run down the hall if they needed anything from the supply room at the end, and run back as fast as they could to get out of there. When cleaning the bathroom in the middle of the hall, they would have to leave the door propped open to avoid what they described as "a smothering feeling."

Had there been foul play in this church sometime in its century of history, something that no one would write about? Why is there the feeling of evil in such a beautiful church, with such a seemingly tranquil recorded history? Early on, one of the church's pastors went to Europe, supposedly for a vacation, and never returned. Is it his spirit people still see today?

The church is not the only haunted building on the property. The pastor's house is also haunted, but everyone who has experienced the activity there agrees that whoever it is, is very friendly. The overall feelings experienced in the house are in stark contrast to those in the church.

The most interesting occurrence in the house happened one day when Ida and her co-worker where cleaning on the second floor. The pastor's wife had left the house, but about an hour later they heard her open the front door and call out to them.

"Girls?" the woman's voice said, prompting both Ida and her co-worker (who had been in different rooms) to stop what they were doing and go to the top of the staircase.

Looking down to the front door area, they didn't see the pastor's wife, so they called out her name. Hearing no response, they went downstairs, but still couldn't find her. They then looked outside and saw that her car was still gone. Looking at each other in amazement, they both agreed that they heard a woman's voice calling them, and that it sounded exactly like the pastor's wife. When she did return an hour later, she confirmed that she had not been back to the house earlier. They chalked it up to a playful spirit just having a little fun.

---

In May 1995, Ida, her husband Jerry, and Jerry's two sons moved into an old farmhouse in Blooming Grove, NY. Interestingly, the house had been owned by the Board family, of which Brewster Board was a member, and he is also connected to the haunted house in Washingtonville (see page 141).

For the most part, the house felt warm and inviting, even the attic and basement. However, there was one exception—a small area in the front yard by the corner of the porch. For some reason this was a very uncomfortable spot, and Ida couldn't even bring herself to walk through it. She didn't say anything about this spot, but later discovered that both boys felt the same way, and also avoided that section of the yard.

The family was very happy in the house, and Ida believed that she would live the rest of her life there with Jerry and the boys. So it was always very upsetting when Jerry would make comments like, "When I'm gone," or say to her that she would live a lot longer than he would.

"Why do you say things like that?" she would ask.

"Because it's true," he would say matter-of-factly, as if he was certain he didn't have long to live and had already accepted his fate. Had he been ill, this attitude might have been understandable, but there wasn't anything wrong with him.

Then came that terrible Saturday when Ida wondered what was taking Jerry so long to get home. He was out on a job towing a trailer, and it shouldn't have taken that long. Then came the call.

Jerry had been bending down by the tow hitch, when the truck slipped out of gear and rolled towards him. He never saw it coming, and his neck was caught between the two bumpers. Even more tragic, his sons, then aged 7 and 10, were there and witnessed to the horrible accident.

Needless to say, it was a full year before the grief-stricken family could even begin to think about living a normal life again. During that year, Ida would sometimes feel as though Jerry's loving presence was with her, but she never saw anything. Then one day one, of the boys came running to her, shouting in excitement.

"Ida, I just saw Dad!" the boy said with a look of happiness, and no hint of fear.

"Where?"

"In the bathroom, shaving," came his reply.

"Do you think you want to see Daddy so badly that you made yourself see him, or was it really him?" Ida asked, wanting to make sure the boy wasn't imagining things.

The boy insisted it was really Jerry, "as clear as day." There was nothing misty or transparent about the figure. Jerry had appeared to be as real and as solid as when he was alive. The boy then admitted that he thought he had seen him on other occasions, but those had been fleeting, ill-defined glimpses. This time, there wasn't a shred of doubt.

Jerry's presence in the house continued to be strong. Then one day, Ida was speaking to a psychic medium in California who said that Jerry wanted to know if it was okay for him to "go over," and that there was an older couple that were like parent figures waiting to help him cross. This information was remarkable for two reasons.

First, Ida said that Jerry never made a move in life without asking her opinion, and the way the psychic worded the request was exactly how Jerry used to speak. Second, a few years before Jerry's passing, an older couple with whom they had been very close friends had also passed away. Though not related, the older man used to call Jerry his son.

So here it was; Jerry was ready to move on, and wanted to make sure that Ida and the boys would be all right. Even though she knew that close feeling of his presence would be lost, she told the psychic to say that it was okay, that everyone would be fine and that Jerry should do what was best for him—whatever that was! From that day on, no one saw Jerry's spirit again, and his almost constant presence was indeed gone. Hopefully, he has found peace on the other side.

While Ida still misses him every day, she finds comfort in knowing that he is content, with loved ones, and in a better place.

---

For a brief period of time, Ida stayed with the friend that she used to work with at the church, in the woman's house built in the 1700s in Chester, NY. Family members and friends had often seen "a lady in white" walking through the house. While Ida never saw this woman, she did hear footsteps coming down the hall to her room every night.

At first she though it must be her friend's children, although their rooms were at the other end of the long hallway. Several times she opened the door and asked who was there, but never received a reply, and never saw anyone. Then one night, as the footsteps began again, she got down on the floor and looked through the slit under the door. Sure enough, there was the dark shadow of two feet right outside her door.

"Okay!" Ida thought, "I have you now!"

Springing to her feet and pulling open the door, she came face to face with...nothing! No one was there, and no one could have gotten away unseen in the second it took to open the door.

There is at least one possible explanation for this activity. Her friend's husband's first wife had died as she exited the bathroom one night on her way back to bed. Her bedroom had been where Ida was sleeping. Was this woman just trying to take the steps in death that she hadn't taken in life? Was she also the "lady in white" that so many people had seen?

Apparently, this lady was not alone, either. One day Ida was working on her computer, and happened to look over toward the open door. A large black cat walked by. No big deal, except the family had no cats. Ida ran into the hall, but couldn't find the cat. It had been perfectly solid, with lifelike detail, but yet it just vanished. When she mentioned this episode to her friend, she just laughed and told her that the first wife had a big, fat, black cat, and it was probably just looking for its former owner.

Just a typical day in a haunted house...

There's also some playfulness to the spirit or spirits of this house. Ida is an artist, and one day as she sat at her desk, something compelled her to turn around and look at a four pound box of clay that sat on a table across the room. Suddenly, the bag of clay "popped off the table and hit the floor." It definitely did not fall over as if off balance, it went up off the table, then out over the floor and dropped.

That same day there was another episode involving of all things, a bag of Fritos! Ida was working at her desk, snacking on a bag of Fritos which sat on a box against the wall. She dropped one of the chips behind the box, and without getting up, reached around behind the box. She felt the chip, but couldn't get it out without standing up and moving the box, and decided not to bother at that moment.

She continued working, and when she turned to grab some more Fritos, there was a single chip lying in the center of the box. She knew it hadn't been there before, and playing a hunch, she reached behind the box, but this time couldn't feel the chip she had dropped. Getting up, she moved the box, but there were no Fritos on the floor. Somehow, the fallen chip had been returned to the top of the box.

Ida could have screamed and run out of the room. Instead, she just thanked the helpful spirit for retrieving her Frito, and went back to work.

Another helpful incident happened one night about a week later when she was working downstairs in the dining room. It was about 3am, and she had just finished and wanted to go upstairs. She had a lot of books and things to carry and planned to turn on the light with her elbow, since her hands were full and she didn't want to make a second trip. As she got about two feet from the stairs (the light switch was at the bottom of the stairs), the light turned on "by itself." Once again, she just smiled and said, "Thanks!"

---

For a while, Ida worked in a bar in Monroe, NY, and often saw the ghost of a man in the kitchen. He was short, chubby, and wore an apron and black shoes. She was never able to see his face, though, as he always ran off when she tried to get a good look at him.

Now she works in another store in Monroe, which is also haunted. (This is a very haunted town!) One evening at closing, the manager was leaning on the checkout counter, when he suddenly jumped up and started yelling something about a boy. He was very agitated, and finally explained that he saw a boy standing several feet away, just staring at him. Of course, they checked the entire store, and found no one.

For no known reason, Ida felt that the boy's name was Joshua. It is now quite common for Josh to be seen and heard by employees and customers. He appears to be about eight years old with dark hair, and is not the least bit threatening, just mischievous. Not surprisingly, he can often be found near the toy section. While his sudden appearances can be momentarily startling, he has become just part of the routine for a woman who has encountered such things just about everywhere she has lived and worked.

---

Does Ida regret having these abilities? Not really, it's just that she would like to be able to use this sixth sense to help people. But perhaps in some way she *is* helping; helping spirits who have not fully crossed over by recognizing and acknowledging their presence. I have seen many times in the past that some spirits just want to make themselves known to the living, to have their stories told, and then they can move on and find peace.

# A House Divided
## Washingtonville, NY

You are never supposed to judge a book by its cover (although the publishing industry would be in big trouble if you didn't!), and the same should go for houses. There's a beautiful nineteenth century house on Route 208 in Washingtonville, New York, that I have been driving past for years and I always thought that whoever lived there was very lucky. Of course, not all luck is good…

In December 2006, I received an email from the owners describing some of the haunted activity that had been taking place in that beautiful house over the past year. I was somewhat surprised, as there is certainly nothing spooky about the appearance or location, but as I have learned time and again, you can't judge a haunted house by its clapboards.

In January of 2007, I arranged to stop by one Sunday evening. I was met by owners Joe and Lucille, and their son, Adam, and daughter, Kim. As is my usual routine, the first step was to obtain as much background information as I could on their experiences and the history of the place before taking a look around. We all sat in a cozy dining area that had no hint of anything paranormal. I didn't let that deceive me, as different rooms of a house can provide vastly different experiences.

Joe and Lucille bought the place in October of 2006. Although the structure clearly looks to be from at least the mid-1800s, the official listing stated that it was built in 1910, because no existing documentation has yet been found to place it earlier. Even after Joe had removed a wall and discovered newspapers dated 1879 that had been used for insulation, the realtor still would not budge on the date, apparently for fear of being accused of misrepresenting a property. For our purposes however, I think we can use common sense and say that the house they bought is most likely about 150 years old.

There had been no advanced warnings that this house might contain restless spirits. There were no paranormal revelations at the closing, and no one made any kind of remarks that would lead one to think that anything out of the ordinary ever took place there. Well, to be honest that's not exactly true…

141

The newspaper from 1878 that Joe found in the wall.

Strange things did go on there, but not of the paranormal variety. Many people in Washingtonville still remember the man who owned the house in the 1950s and 60s. He was a colorful character, to say the least, and came to be known as "Cape Man," as he strode about town in a cape, smoking cigarettes through a long holder. In a quiet community still dominated by farms, he must have stuck out like the proverbial sore thumb. He died in 1979, although Cape Man may not yet have left the building, but more on that later.

The first episode of an unusual nature experienced by the new owners occurred during the extensive renovations. The place had been in pretty bad shape, and the plans were to fix it up and open a café on the first floor, while their daughter would live on the second floor. Joe was working alone late one night in one of the bedrooms on the second floor. He was on his hands and knees cleaning paint chips off the floor (the windows had all been painted shut and required a lot of scraping), when a sudden icy cold breeze swept over him.

The windows in the house were closed, he was not in front of a doorway, and he stopped working to try to figure out what had just happened. He had always been skeptical about ghosts, and he wanted a rational explanation for this inexplicable sudden cold air mass that just blew by. However, before he could think for long, the sound of gushing water hit his ears.

"Oh great!" Joe thought. "Now a pipe has burst!"

He explained that this was not the sound of water coming out of a small diameter sink faucet, but more like rushing full force from a large tub faucet. Running to the nearest bathroom, he found that all the plumbing was intact and not so much as a drop of water was leaking. He searched other rooms and couldn't find any signs of the burst pipe. Then the gushing sound stopped as quickly and mysteriously as it had begun, but even if there hadn't been a real water leak, the damage was done—to Joe's nerves. The icy air that had blown by him, coupled with the inexplicable water sound was all he could take that night. He freely admitted he was scared and quickly went home.

Shortly after this episode, Lucille was working inside the house when there was a knock on the door. A short, elderly lady stood on the porch smiling. When Lucille asked if she could be of any assistance, the woman politely informed her, "You know this isn't a quiet house."

Puzzled, Lucille asked what she meant, and the visitor explained that she had lived in the area for many years, and had experienced strange things in this house, including seeing the ghosts of cats prowling around. The woman could obviously see the look of surprise and concern on Lucille's face, so she quickly added, "Don't worry, there's nothing bad here. It's just a very...active house." With that, the lady turned and left. Lucille has no idea who she was, but I would bet she wasn't a regular member of Welcome Wagon.

Another local man who worked in the house about ten years ago also told Lucille of strange things happening. He described hearing "lots of footsteps" throughout the house when no one else was there. It was beginning to look like this was a genuine haunted house!

Not that Joe needed any further convincing, but he did have another bizarre experience. He was on the bottom floor (at ground level, beneath the main first floor) with his cousin in a room that used to be the kitchen (with a fireplace and built-in baking oven that is obviously from the 1800s, but don't get me started on that bogus 1910 date again). Joe thought he saw a dark shape or shadow move across the room. This sighting was accompanied by another cold mass of air. The door to the room was shut, but the latch began to jiggle and rattle as if someone on the other side was trying to open it. Both men fully expected someone to come walking in, but the door never opened, and when they checked, no one was there.

In fact, it most likely was someone on the other side—of death, that is.

Another incident with a door happened to Adam. During Christmastime of 2006, he was selling trees on the lawn, so he tried to remain aware of potential thieves. One night he awoke to hear a diesel truck, and couldn't tell if the truck was in the street or on the property. Putting his ear close to the bedroom door, he held his breath and strained to hear what was going on.

A moment later, there was a loud "BAM" on the door near his head, as if someone had pounded on the other side of the door with his fist. Adam jumped back into bed, not caring if someone was out there stealing all of the Christmas trees! (Fortunately, it had just been a truck passing down the road.)

Kim and her five-year-old daughter have probably experienced the most activity, as they live there. Footsteps up the staircases, across the attic, and back and forth through the halls have become so commonplace they tend to ignore them now. Knocking on the doors and rattling the handles is also a common occurrence, most often just after Kim has closed and locked her door. It's as if someone doesn't like being locked out.

The children's playroom.

Kim's daughter often talks about seeing a woman and her young daughter, and can't understand why no one else sees them. She even calls them by name, Abigail and Shelby, and doesn't seem at all concerned that they aren't alive. She plays with the little girl, and very much enjoys being in the front bedroom where children tend to gravitate. Lucille said that on many occasions children visiting the family or coming to the café with their parents would go off on their own and find their way to that particular room. Can these children also see Shelby, or is something else drawing them there?

The kitchen is also the scene of inexplicable activity. One day when Lucille was cleaning up the ice cream area, stainless steel containers started coming off the counter as if pushed. Another time in that same location, a spoon took off and flew across the room. Lucille wasn't about to take that kind of nonsense, so she scolded the offending spirit, telling it to knock it off before someone got hurt. From that day everything was quiet—and remained in place—in that one area, at least.

The area of the kitchen where objects were flying through the air.

Joe had a similar experience in the main kitchen. A loaf of bread fell off a shelf, which didn't mean anything strange was going on, as it could simply have been sitting on the edge and finally fell. However, the second Joe bent down to pick up the bread, a cup came off the drying rack and hit the floor. Now that was odd, because the drying rack has a raised rim, so something would have had to lift the cup up and over the rim to make it fall.

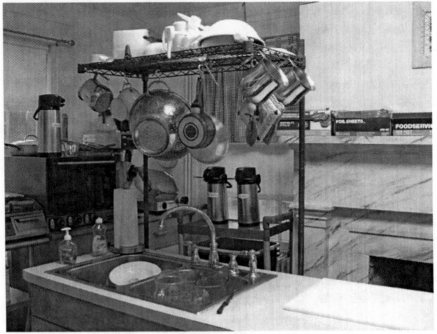

The drying rack in the kitchen.

At this house, paranormal encounters are not limited to family members. After renovations were complete and the restaurant opened, some sensitive patrons began telling Lucille that they saw spirits in the house, and quite a few at that. One woman even claimed to see the apparition of a very large man. "Cape Man" had been a very tall, heavyset man, so it was suspected that perhaps his spirit is among those still in residence.

While the activity all seems to be non-threatening, there is nonetheless a distinct difference in the types of feelings generated in certain parts of the house. The activity in the main part of the house where the original families would have lived feels friendly, and perhaps just a bit mischievous. However, the side that once held the servants' quarters has been given the official designation of being "creepy." It is unpleasant at the least, and just menacing enough to make certain family members avoid those rooms. (The room where Joe had the first encounter with the cold air and sound of gushing water is in the "creepy" section.)

Perhaps the most dramatic encounter of all also took place in one of these former servant's bedrooms. Adam's friend, Tom, was going to spend the night, and as he was a "100% non-believer," he had no qualms about sleeping in one of the creepy bedrooms. However, his "non-believer" status was about to change, in a few rapid heartbeats...

Tom was in bed, the door to the room was closed, and he turned off the light. Not much more than a minute later, Adam heard his friend shouting, "Whoa, whoa...WHOA!!!" At first he assumed his friend was just kidding around, but when Tom started shouting, "Oh my god," over and over again, in obvious distress, Adam ran to the door.

Calling to Tom, Adam asked what was wrong, and told him to come out of the room. A moment later Tom opened the door, and the look on his face showed that this was no joke. When questioned, he wouldn't reveal what had transpired. Clearly agitated and somewhat annoyed that something had happened that was beyond his set of beliefs, Tom simply slipped into denial and declared that he must have been dreaming, and insisted on going back in the room.

Adam explained that it was unlikely that whatever happened had been a dream, because Tom had only just turned out the light. This appeared to be a surprise to Tom, for if his dream theory had any validity, he would have necessarily needed the time to fall into a deep sleep. He insisted on going back in that bedroom, and no imaginary spirits were going to shake his resolve—a brave and rational stance, unless of course, there is one genuine spirit to shake that resolve.

Several minutes later, Tom quietly exited the bedroom once again, went to the room where Adam was spending the night and said he preferred to sleep on the couch in there instead. This time Adam insisted on finding out what had gone on, and Tom relented and told his story.

Shortly after getting into bed (the first time) and turning off the light, Tom saw the apparition of a man by the door. The phantom man then floated across the room and sat down in a chair next to the bed—while Tom shouted in shock and disbelief. He hadn't told about what he had seen because it all seemed so impossible. The second time he went to bed in that room he heard heavy footsteps walking around the bed. At least he was spared the sight of an apparition this time, but it was a small consolation and he had enough. Seeing—and hearing—is believing, and Tom was a changed man.

The chair (center) where the apparition "took a seat."

From that night, he became fascinated with the possibility of paranormal activity in that house, and he and Adam devised a plan. They placed strings across doorways to see if any of them would be broken by the unseen residents. When they returned later on, all the strings were intact, but one was "wiggling" as if a breeze was blowing. There was no breeze, and all of the other strings were motionless. Encouraged, Adam started asking a series of questions, and as if in response, this one string would move more vigorously. At one point, the string really "jumped," sending the two startled men running. It was a simple, low-tech experiment, but it produced some very interesting results.

Adam was now really enthusiastic about trying to communicate with the spirits of the house, and several days later he set up another string experiment. This time nothing unusual happened, until he went to take down the strings. He just couldn't untie the knot at the end of one of the strings, so he took out the folding knife he always keeps on his belt. This is a knife he has used just about every day for ten years and he never once cut himself.

Now here he was just going to cut a small knot in a little string and somehow he cut himself so badly he "almost sliced the top off" his finger! Was this a careless accident, a mere coincidence, or was it something more ominous—a warning, perhaps, to stop messing around with things he didn't understand? In any event, Adam admitted that the incident caused him to be much less enthusiastic about trying to contact the dead.

After listening to the family members' stories, Adam gave me a tour of the house. We began at the lower level, where I had my first odd sensation. It was in the old kitchen (where Joe and his cousin had the encounter), and while I couldn't ascribe the feeling to a male or female, or any type of personality, there was a distinct presence. After investigating haunted places for all these years, you learn to respect these feelings, even if they can never constitute documented evidence.

The former kitchen on the ground floor. There had been plans to turn it into a barber shop, hence the great old chairs. (Adam is on the left.)

I decided to put a tri-field EMF meter in the center of the room and set up a camcorder to tape in infrared while we continued on through the rest of the house. When I checked the tape a few days later, I found that sounds from living people moving in the house made it impossible to say if there were any paranormal sounds. However, on numerous occasions the EMF meter alarm did go off—indicating passing electromagnetic fields of unknown origin.

There was an amusing incident as I was setting up the equipment here. The tri-field meter has something of a screeching alarm, and it takes a moment or two to adjust it and let it settle down before it is silent. I had just finished when Joe came hurrying into the basement.

"Are you all right?" he asked with concern.

I replied that I was fine, and asked if there was a problem. He said that the people upstairs thought they heard a woman scream in the basement, and he was worried that something had happened to me. Adam and I looked at each other in surprise, because we hadn't heard anything. The mystery was finally solved when it was determined that it was the meter alarm that had sounded like a woman in distress. Nonetheless, I thanked Joe for gallantly rushing to my rescue.

On the first floor in the front room that was part of the café, Adam explained that one day his girlfriend was looking at the curved glass display case that held the cakes and pastries. She could see her own reflection, and suddenly saw the reflection of a man standing right behind her. Quickly turning, she found that no one was there. Turning back, the reflection in the glass was gone.

While other visitors to the house had also witnessed or sensed a presence on the first floor, the encounters had basically been brief and benign, just little reminders that the house was still occupied. Yet, these rooms on the first floor did not feel uncomfortable, and Adam confirmed that no one had ever experienced anything unpleasant in this area of the house.

The kitchen area had so many appliances that were generating their own EMF fields that it was impossible to determine if anything unusual was going on with the meters. And as I only had a couple of camcorders with me, I decided that this section of the house would have to wait until next time for a "stake out."

We headed upstairs where Adam showed me his sister's room. I tried to take a picture of the door (upon which something knocks and bangs with regularity), and three times I pressed the shutter button on my camera, but the camera did not respond. Finally, on the fourth try I was able to take a picture. The camera had been fine to his point, and had no problems the rest of the night, but for some odd reason it was reluctant to take a picture of the door.

There were high EMF readings throughout the room, particularly in the center. We tested near the ceiling and the floor to see if perhaps electrical wiring was the cause of the high electromagnetic field, but the readings were near zero above and below, and from side to side, and I commented about the difference in readings a distance of a foot or two made. So how do you generate a field in midair with no surrounding readings? Sounds like something paranormal to me. Perhaps a presence was right there in front of us?

Next we went into the children's playroom that was filled with toys. This is the room that children are drawn to, but before you say, well of course, because it's filled with toys, consider the fact that children who have never been to the house before and who have no prior knowledge make a beeline up the stairs and right to this room.

There were extremely high EMF readings here—too high to be considered paranormal—and indeed I was able to trace the source to electrical lines on the outside corner of the house. That doesn't mean that there isn't paranormal energy in this room, it just means that like the kitchen that is filled with appliances generating their own EM fields, you have to be careful to consider normal sources before jumping to any conclusions.

Then we crossed the wide hall to the old servant's section of the house. Adam showed me the room where his friend saw that apparition, and pointed out the chair where it "sat." The next room over was the small storage room where Joe had the first experience of the cold air and sound of running water. Neither of these rooms had any unusual readings, at first, but more on that later.

We went up into the attic which had the original old hand hewn beams, again clearly older than 1910. There were also massive silver air conditioning ducts snaking across the floor, and I commented that it was like some alien creature. So we already had ghosts and now aliens, but would there be any other surprises? Unfortunately, yes, but not of the paranormal variety. In the darkness I couldn't see that there was an opening in the floor where one of the ducts went to a lower level, like the gaping jaws of a hungry creature. One second I was on my feet, the next my leg had been swallowed up to the hip down into the floor.

Fortunately, I was not cut and there were no broken bones, only wounded pride. Of course, as I was plunging my first thought was to save the equipment, so I instinctively lifted it up to protect it, and everything was okay. (The thought of dropping my equipment and using my hands to break my fall didn't enter my head. At least I have my priorities straight...) This time Adam came to my rescue and pulled me out of the hole. I brushed a hundred years of dust off my leg and we continued.

The old beams in the attic.

One thing I noticed, after I was back on my feet, was that it was a very sturdy floor, not subject to generating creaking sounds. Footsteps and other sounds are often heard in the attic, particularly over Kim's bedroom, but I wasn't able to find any loose floorboards that could provide a natural explanation for these sounds.

Also, as we sat quietly by the top of the attic stairs, the EMF meter was reading a steady 1.1, so I assumed it was some normal electrical background level. However, quite suddenly, and for no apparent reason, it dropped down to 0.1 and stayed there. This is a very reliable and accurate meter, and this became another small, yet inexplicable mystery. Inconsistencies such as this may not in of itself be anything startling, but if they begin to grow in number it is worth taking notice.

Joe joined us in our attic stake out, but nothing more of note occurred there. The term "not cooperating" was used to describe the evening to this point, but I know you can't expect dramatic results on every investigation. While we didn't hear any footsteps or banging on doors, I was not disappointed in the curious EMF readings, or odd sensations in a few locations. And, the night was not over.

The three of us went to the bedroom where the apparition had appeared to Adam's friend, closed the door, and sat quietly in the dark. Several minutes passed with nothing unusual. Then there was a brief change, a moment of deeper darkness that caught my attention. I know your eyes can play tricks on you sometimes in very low light conditions, but I could have sworn that the thin line of light around the doorframe went black, as if someone had passed in front of the door and blocked the light in the hall. Unfortunately, neither Joe nor Adam had been looking at the door so they didn't notice anything. It would have been great if someone else had seen it, but I am still quite certain of what I saw.

We waited patiently for a while, but everything was quiet, and I didn't see anymore interruptions in the light. I rarely go the route of trying to antagonize spirits, but I decided to chide them just a bit, saying that they were scared to make themselves known now that we were waiting for them, and that we weren't afraid. Several minutes passed and I stated that this was their last chance, that if they didn't make some sign I would leave. Then I specifically challenged them to make the readings on the EMF meter change, not really expecting any response, and suddenly there was a brief spike of energy, then another.

Continuing to take that tack, I said, "We aren't convinced by just that-" I started to say, but stopped when the readings went up again and held.

"All right, maybe we are starting to get convinced," I said with a laugh. "That's interesting. That's pretty good."

Experiencing paranormal phenomena is always amazing, but the most impressive experiences are the interactive ones. I challenged something to create energy that could be detected on the EMF meter, and lo and behold, it did. Very cool! And it was to get even more astonishing.

When the readings declined, I tried a few questions to see if we could get specific information. I asked if it was a male presence, but nothing happened. I then asked if it was a female presence, and there was the slightest flicker of a response, but not strong enough to be definitive. Then came the kicker—I asked it the spirit was unhappy, and the instant I said the word "unhappy" the readings shot up. They quickly returned to zero, and as I was explaining to Joe and Adam what had happened when I said "unhappy" there was a second spike of energy the instant I repeated the word. I then admitted I was covered with goose bumps. This was very exciting stuff.

Joe then asked the million dollar question. "If they're unhappy, why do they stay here? Why don't they just leave?"

Makes sense doesn't it? If you're unhappy with a situation, walk away from it. The only way I could respond was that for some reason ghosts are stuck in these situations, and it appears as though the negative energies of their anger, hatred, jealousy, fears, etc., are the very things keeping them trapped within these unnatural situations.

Hey, kind of sounds like life, doesn't it? How many people are unhappy with their jobs, spouses, and lives in general, but put up with the misery year after year, rather then expending some energy to get themselves to happier and more satisfying places? I don't want to preach on this soap box too long, but how can we blame ghosts for remaining in bad situations, when the living are guilty of the same inaction?

I tried again asking if it was a male or female presence, but there were no responses. We sat quietly for a while longer, and the meter occasionally showed high readings, that quickly disappeared as suddenly as they appeared. It was very unusual, but gave us no further answers, so we decided to move on to the smaller room where Joe had first experienced the cold air and sound of running water.

At first there wasn't anything happening, then simultaneously we all felt very cold. The goose bumps were back, and the meter alarm suddenly squealed to announce the presence of some detectable energy that was not there previously. (The three of us sat on the floor, and the meter was on a table several feet away so our own movements and natural energy from our bodies could not influence the readings.) I heard some odd sounds, but with other people in the house at the time, I couldn't say that they weren't made by the living.

We waited for quite a while, but nothing more happened. I had the infrared camcorder in the hall, and decided to aim it into the room and watch the viewfinder to see if anything was going on in wavelengths beyond our ability to see. Joe and Adam were sitting with their backs against the far wall, so I pointed the camera toward them. Almost immediately there was a small white spot that moved from right to left, directly in front of them. As I was describing what I saw and explaining that dust could cause such spots, there were several more.

The door to the room was shut, the window was closed, and there wasn't any discernable source of a breeze, especially a breeze strong enough to make dust particles move so quickly, and in the same right to left path. I always struggle with defining these bizarre white spots and my rational mind wants to ascribe them all to the realm of natural airborne particles, but on the other hand, my curious nature asks why dust should act like that in a closed room. I will simply have to report that I observed them, they were recorded on tape, and their origin is unknown.

I stopped the tape at that point to show Adam what I was talking about. His reaction was something along the lines of, "Whoa! That ain't no piece of dust." I then showed it to Joe, who observed that they did have specific directions, and pointed out that they couldn't possibly be from passing car lights. Adam then stated he had actually *seen* one of the moving small spots of light with his own eyes as he sat on the floor. If that was the case, then truly they weren't "no pieces of dust."

They returned to the floor and I continued recording. Minutes passed, and no more lights appeared. I commented that if dust was swirling around the room, why wasn't it doing so now? Then I opened the door and moved the camcorder into the hall so I could get a better view of the room. The open door should have increased the air circulation in the room, but still nothing else appeared.

Adam checking the EMF readings in the small room.

We left Joe alone in the room, while Adam and I returned to the basement. Still taping in infrared, Adam and I watched the camcorder screen and saw quite a flurry of those white lights zipping around, and there was one that really sparkled. Then they abruptly stopped. We tried to see if we could duplicate the fast moving spots by stirring up the air and stamping our feet on the floor to stir up dust, but not so much as a speck appeared.

We spent some time in the basement, but nothing else happened. We checked on Joe, and he also had nothing more to report. That was the end of that night's investigation, but there was enough tantalizing evidence to convince me to return.

I did return with Mike one cold evening in February, and Adam was there to meet us. For Mike's edification, we began with a walkthrough. Although he did not know any of the specific details of the house's activity, Mike did get a distinct feeling when he walked into the old kitchen on the first floor, just as I had. He also felt a shift in the feeling between the two sides of the house on the top floor, the division between the former servants' quarters and the family's section. This difference has been experienced by many people.

We set up camcorders and equipment in the old kitchen in the basement, the new kitchen on the first floor, and the bedroom on the servants' side of the house where the apparition had been seen. Mike sat inside the bedroom, while Adam and I stood out in the hall. I had wanted to reproduce the string experiment that Adam had conducted, but all he could find was a length of ribbon, which he stretched across the doorway and attached to either side of the frame.

We stood quietly for a while, then Adam posed a challenge to the spirits to make the ribbon move. There was some definite movement, a slight flutter that may or may not have been caused by a breeze that we couldn't detect. Then there were sounds on the floor below us, as if someone was moving around. Had this been the last investigation with all of the people in the house, I wouldn't have thought twice, but this time we were alone.

A moment later Mike announced that there were some fluctuations in the digital EMF meter he was holding. Then Adam said, "Just give us a sign of your presence." With that the ribbon moved more vigorously, and the tri-field EMF meter alarm began to sound. It all only lasted a few seconds, then the ribbon became still and the energy fluctuations stopped. We waited for more signs, and I decided to see if I could "encourage" whatever was present to repeat the activity that had just occurred.

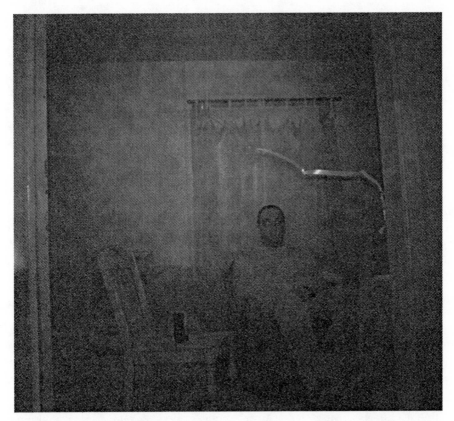

The ribbon stretched across the doorway. Mike is sitting in the "ghost chair."

"If you have the energy to become visible, you should be able to move the ribbon and make the meter go off."

Unfortunately, the ribbon didn't move again, and the meter didn't go off, but I was not disappointed, because an instant later there was a very loud banging sound from somewhere below us on the first floor, or perhaps the basement. All three of us heard it clearly. I had challenged whatever was there for one type of sign, but they provided another, and it was a rather convincing sign at that.

Adam had hoped that the ribbon would jump dramatically, but a loud, almost threatening banging sound wasn't half bad, either. A minute or so later there was also a rush of cold air coming out from the room that was equally impressive, and spine tingling! Mike didn't experience the cold that Adam and I did out in the hall, but he was having problems of his own inside the bedroom, and they were about to get worse.

The unpleasant feelings experienced by many people in that room were gradually affecting Mike with increasing intensity. Adam and I decided to join Mike in the room and close the door. I then posed another challenge, only this time it was to Mike to sit in the chair by the window where the apparition had parked its non-corporeal rear end. Never one to shy from a challenge, Mike took a seat. And, never one to resist trying to stir things up, he began to accuse the spirits of "being afraid to come out."

Guess what? They weren't.

Almost immediately, Mike began to feel pressure on his forehead. His hand moved back and forth across his head as if trying to remove something, but nothing was physically touching him. Still, the pressure increased to the point where his head was actually being pushed backward. The feelings accompanying this bizarre force were equally uncomfortable—bad feelings of strong negative emotions, a headache, and nausea. Within a few minutes it all became too much and he had to get out of the chair.

To get a better perspective on the entire room, I once again opened the door and stood in the hall. I aimed the camcorder into the room and kept an eye on the small screen. The lights were all out and I was intent on watching for any activity in the infrared spectrum. Suddenly, an unsettling feeling crept over me.

"This is going to sound clichéd, but I feel like I'm being watched…from behind."

If you have never experienced anything of this nature, this may sound strange, but the presence "felt" male. Often, there are no distinctive characteristics, but on occasion you can sense gender, approximate age (e.g. child, adult, elderly person), as well as other personality traits, and this entity felt like a male—a very angry male.

"I think you really pissed off something," I added, referring to Mike's attempt to stir up things.

The feeling diminished, but lingered, and we decided to move to the other side of the house, the "good" side, and went first to the room that was filled with toys. There were some very high EMF readings again in this room, but as we had previously discovered there are electrical lines running outside along the corner of the house, so it is impossible to determine if any paranormal energies are part of these readings. However, two events occurred here that were clearly not normal.

The first happened to Mike when he opened the closet door. After several moments, a mass of cold air came out of the closet and passed through him. Now I know closets can be chilly as they aren't heated, but if cold air was to come out of a closet, shouldn't it do so as soon as the door is opened? Also, Mike felt the walls and contents inside the closet and they were all about the same temperature as objects in the room, so there was not a substantial difference between the closet and the room. So, where did the cold air come from? And where was it going?

The second event is still one I question, but only because it was so strange and startling that it is hard to believe. Mike was talking about the spirits of the mother and daughter that Adam's niece claimed to be able to see, and recalled that the young girl had named them. He remembered one name, Abigail, but couldn't come up with the other name. Just as I was starting to say that name, I could have sworn a heard a young girl's voice behind me say, "Shelby."

I immediately asked if Mike or Adam had heard the voice, but they hadn't. I then checked the digital recorder I was holding to see if the phantom voice had been captured. Unfortunately, it had not. But what was recorded was my voice responding to Mike as I said, "Sh-Shelby." No, I hadn't picked up a stuttering habit, the hesitation in my voice was the result of being distracted by hearing the little girl speak at the same time.

But why hadn't anyone else heard it, and why hadn't it been recorded? Could the voice have come from someone out on the street, and I only interpreted it as saying Shelby? Or, had I simply imagined the whole thing? While I have to consider all of the possibilities, I would still have to say that I believe I heard a little girl's voice speaking just a few feet behind me.

We continued on throughout the house, and found that the basement room that used to be the original kitchen still had inexplicably high EMF readings that came and went. There is a distinct presence in that room, as well, one that is different from the others upstairs. While it is slightly unsettling, it is nothing like the hostile spirit in the servants' quarters, or the benign female entities on the other side of the house.

Toward the end of the investigation, we all agreed that the most active place was that servant's bedroom, and we wanted to spend some more time there. Mike was brave enough to sit in the chair again, although not for very long. He realized that the chair was in front of the window, and wondered if whatever had been pushing him, was actually trying to get him out of the house, via the window, although at no point was this even a remote possibility. Still, you have to give the spirit credit for trying!

He described the presence as "menacing" and the tension increased by the minute, once again resulting in unpleasant physical feelings such as nausea. Generally, one would shy away from such a situation, but I decided I also needed to take my turn in the spiritual "hot seat." While I didn't feel as though I was being pushed or threatened, it became uncomfortable, and my scalp and forehead began to tingle.

"You know what? I don't want to sit in this chair either," I said after just a few minutes. "Maybe it's suggestion, but it's feeling really weird."

That only left Adam to try the chair, which he sat down in with confidence. This was the first time he had ever felt comfortable in that room, and I suggested that perhaps it was because Mike "was running block" for him that night. Unfortunately, the energy that had been directed at Mike for most of the evening shifted toward Adam after he sat in the chair. With more of a "well, it was nice while it lasted" attitude than one of fear, Adam also got up from the chair and sat in a different part of the room.

That made it Spooky Chair 3-Ghost Investigators 0.

One could very well argue that it was all a case of the power of suggestion, but by simply moving to another seat in the room the feeling subsided. I personally believe that there are at last two things going on in this bedroom. First, there is some residual energy of a past event, energy that is concentrated in a line from the door to the window and is most potent around that chair. Second, I believe there is a very angry male presence, someone who directs his anger at other men. I came to this conclusion in part because while the entity has been experienced by many, it does seem particularly intent on bothering, and perhaps even "attacking," other men.

What terrible act had been committed in this room long ago that has left such an unpleasant energy, and a trapped spirit that won't let it go? Is it still a force so potent that it can harm the living? Even if it is unable to cause physical injury, it has clearly been successful inflicting psychological damage, even with brief exposure. My recommendation? No one should ever sleep in that bedroom, especially men.

As for the rest of this beautiful house, if you don't mind a few footsteps and noises, and the occasional apparition, it would make a fine home or business. The café has since closed, but at the time of this writing another restaurant was slated to try its luck there.

So far, very little information about this house and its occupants has been uncovered. It would be nice to at least establish the age of the structure, and of course, it would be even better if we could unravel the mysteries of the angry man, the mother and daughter, and the other untold number of spirits that will not leave.

From the former café, I will only say arrivederci, not goodbye, as this is one case that will always be open until answers are found and the dead find peace in this house divided.

To order books, get info, and share your haunting,
contact the Ghost Investigator through:

www.ghostinvestigator.com

Or write to:

Linda Zimmermann
P.O. Box 192
Blooming Grove, NY 10914

Or send email to:

linda@gotozim.com

Copy this page to use for your own ghost hunt. If you know of a haunted site you think should be considered for an upcoming book, please contact me at:

P.O. Box 192, Blooming Grove, NY, 10914

www.ghostinvestigator.com

*Field Report*

**Date:**            **Location:**

**Time In:**            **Weather:**

**Names of People Interviewed:**

**Equipment: Camera** ☐ **Video** ☐ **Audio Recorder**
            ☐ **Thermometer**        **Other:**

**Experiences:   Sounds** ☐   **Odors** ☐    **Cold Spots** ☐

**Visuals** ☐ **Touch/Sensations** ☐ **Movement** ☐

**Details (Attach extra sheet if necessary):**

**Time Out:**            **Total Time on Site:**

**Conclusions:**

**Prepared and Signed by:**

**Witness(es):**

# Other books by Linda Zimmermann

## *Dead Center*
### *A Ghost Hunter Novel*

When one of the country's largest shopping centers is built in Virginia, rumors abound that the place is haunted by ghosts of Civil War soldiers. Ghost hunter Sarah Brooks must uncover the truth, and come face to face with the restless spirits that walk through the *Dead Center*.

*Okay, Sarah Brooks. This is what you do*, she said to herself. *This is who you are.*

Closing her eyes, Sarah spun around and counted to three. When she opened her eyes, she had to clamp her hand over her mouth to stifle a scream. There was a pale, misty shape of a man drawing closer. It was like an image being projected into a fog, and it rippled, wavered, then slowly began to take on a more defined shape. The wounded man behind her screamed as if Death himself was coming to take him...

*Ghost Investigator Volume 1:* Hauntings of the Hudson Valley
*Ghost Investigator Volume 2:* From Gettysburg to Lizzie Borden
*Ghost Investigator Volume 3*
*Ghost Investigator Volume 4:* Ghosts of New York and New Jersey
*Ghost Investigator Volume 5:* From Beyond the Grave
*Ghost Investigator Volume 6:* Dark Shadows

Printed in the United States
94147LV00004B/64-69/A